LEAVING A LEGACY

LEAVING A LEGACY

Sustaining Family Unity, Faith, and Wealth

DAN T. GARRETT
& TIM WOODROOF

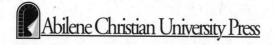
Abilene Christian University Press

All profits from the sale of this book will be donated to support:

Your Legacy Foundation
1355 Stoneham Street
Superior, CO 80027
www.yourlegacyfoundation.org

(This foundation provides scholarships for training nonprofit staff in
Heritage and Legacy Planning.)

LEAVING A LEGACY
Sustaining Family Unity, Faith, and Wealth

ACU
PRESS

Copyright 2014 by Dan T. Garrett

ISBN 978-0-89112-492-4 | LCCN 2013042990

Printed in the United States of America

Scripture quotations, unless otherwise noted, are from The Holy Bible, New International Version.
Copyright 1984, International Bible Society. Used by permission of Zondervan Publishers.

LIBRARY OF CONGRESS CATALOGING-IN-PUBLICATION DATA
Garrett, Dan T., 1945-
  Leaving a legacy : sustaining family unity, faith, and wealth / Dan T. Garrett, Tim Woodroof.
    pages cm
  ISBN 978-0-89112-492-4
1. Families--Religious aspects--Christianity. 2. Parenting--Religious aspects--Christianity. 3. Child
rearing--Religious aspects--Christianity. 4. Families--Religious life. 5. Legacies. 6. Wealth--Religious
aspects--Christianity. I. Woodroof, Tim, 1955- II. Title.
  BT707.7.G37 2014
  248'.6--dc23
                                                                                          2013042990

Cover design by Rick Gibson | Interior text design by Sandy Armstrong, Strong Design

For information contact:
Abilene Christian University Press
1626 Campus Court
Abilene, Texas 79601

1-877-816-4455 | www.acupressbooks.com

14 15 16 17 18 19 / 7 6 5 4 3 2 1

Publication of this book was made possible by
The ZOE Donor Advised Fund

To my family:

Donna, my bride of forty-three years—your unconditional love sustained me in the dark days, and your smile and encouragement brought sunshine to all my days.

My sons Grant, Mack, and John—a father could not be more proud of his sons.

My beautiful daughters-in-law—you are the answer to prayers long ago.

My current and future grandchildren—may this legacy be a blessing.

—Dan T. Garrett

To Sarah, James, and Jonathan:

My children . . . my friends . . . my companions on the road to tomorrow.

—Tim Woodroof

TABLE OF CONTENTS

FOREWORD

I met Dan Garrett at a professional development event in Portland, Oregon in 2009. I had the opportunity to interview him about the people and events that shaped his life and, in a few short moments, felt a deep personal connection. It was obvious that we shared a common faith and many core values. Dan possesses a rare combination of a pastor's heart, a leader's vision, and a counselor's discernment.

Over the past few decades, Dan has met with many dozens, if not hundreds, of affluent individuals and has helped them to recall their own life-shaping events and people. Sharing memories takes the form of stories. As a trained wealth counselor, Dan helps people discover through sharing their stories how their core values and character qualities have emerged over time. Values and character are the things that shape our vision (the way we want our future to be). And what we want our future to be influences our behavior which, over time, determines our legacy. It is an amazing gift to be able to see how the key events and people in our past have shaped who we are today. It is perhaps even more powerful to understand that we can proactively apply these same principles to leave a legacy, especially leaving a lasting positive influence on our families.

So how do we do this? The traditional advisor community is not trained to help families leave a legacy. Someone once said, "Estate planning does a great job of preparing the money for the heirs but it does nothing to prepare the heirs for the money." It is tragic that so many people spend so little time working on transferring their values and life lessons to the next generation. Part of the reason for this is that so little has been written about how to do it.

Thankfully, now Dan Garrett and Tim Woodroof have given us the tools we need to capture and preserve these memories, stories, and life lessons for our families. *Leaving a Legacy* is a practical how-to guide that that all of us can use to identify and celebrate the people and experiences that have shaped our lives. I can't wait to employ the practical ideas it contains with my own family.

David W. Holaday
Wealth Design Consultants, LLC
Carmel, Indiana

ACKNOWLEDGMENTS

We place *Leaving a Legacy* in your hands with a great sense of the debt to Perry Cochell and Rodney Zeeb. Their book *Beating the Midas Curse* (Heritage Institute Press, 2005) is the foundation on which our work was built. Many of the ideas presented here (indeed, many of the *words*) come from Cochell's and Zeeb's book.

Beating the Midas Curse, however, has its own context. It grew out of two decades of experience, research, and interactions with families by the Heritage Institute. Cochell, Zeeb, and their colleagues at the Heritage Institute studied, developed, and tested the principles that eventually became *Beating the Midas Curse*. And so our debt extends to the Heritage Institute and its partners. Without their pioneering efforts, the present book would not have been written.

The contribution we hope to make with *Leaving a Legacy* is to expand the discussion of legacy issues among people of faith. In using *Midas Curse* when talking with families about legacy issues, we were constantly reminded (in our own discussions and by the comments of others) of the *spiritual* principles and implications inherent in these ideas. Drawing out these spiritual dimensions was not Perry's and Rodney's focus as they wrote *Midas Curse*.

But it is *our* focus. In this work, you will find frequent references to the teachings of Jesus, lessons drawn from his parables, and spiritual principles about living in a material world. Many of the families we work with are—at their core—families of faith. Faith shapes their values and perspectives. Faith motivates and sustains them. We thought such families might appreciate thinking more deeply about biblical insights for passing along both their valuables and their values.

—Dan T. Garrett and Tim Woodroof

WHAT WILL YOU PASS ON?

Whether by choice or by chance, you will leave something behind for those who follow.

It may be great or small, valuable or meager, honorable or disreputable, calculated in dollars or measured in character. You may wrap what you leave in a will or safety-deposit box . . . or in the hearts and attitudes of your heirs. Your impact on the future may take the form of material wealth, or the habit of generosity, or an example of faith, or the scars of broken relationships. You may pass your baton to people who love you or resent you or (worst of all, perhaps) do not think of you at all.

But whatever survives you when you are gone will be your legacy. You are responsible for the echoes of your living, for whether others are blessed (or cursed) by the ripples you set in motion, for whether those stranded by your ebbing tide are prepared to navigate the reefs and shallows left behind.

No matter what you accomplish or fail to accomplish . . . no matter your virtues or sins . . . no matter how deliberate or negligent you may be about the future, one thing is certain: you will leave something behind.

The question is not *whether*. The question is *who* . . . and *what* . . . and *how* . . . and *why*.

Who are your true heirs? *What* will you leave behind? *How* will you transfer yourself to the future? And *why* do you want to make an offering to the future to begin with?

These are hard questions, rarely asked. They require us to think carefully about what we truly value, to explore how the things we hold precious can effectively be placed into the lives of those who are precious to us, and to honestly face the issue of what motivates us and what will motivate our heirs.

The underlying premise of this book is that the values you live by are your most important asset, and the greatest inheritance your heirs will receive has less to do with valuables than with wisdom.

Fortunately, passing on a legacy can be *facilitated* by valuables. In preparing those you love to be good *heirs*, you have an opportunity to prepare them to be good *people*.

CHAPTER ONE

HANDING OFF THE FUTURE

Leaving a Legacy

In all the dark world, through all the dark deeds over all the dark days, behind all the dark lives bent beneath their dark burdens, he could yet see flickers of the Father's love—glimmers of the Father's light—in the ways of parents with their children.

He'd noticed it before: in the eager, ardent way parental hands reached for a child's head or shoulder or fingers; in the way parental eyes tended to lock and linger on one face in a passing knot of kids; in the voices of fathers crying mercy for sick daughters; in the tears of mothers mourning only sons.

He saw it now as parents guided their wee ones with protective gestures, through fissures in the crowds, to places near the front where shorter spectators might see and hear. He saw it as they unwrapped bread and olives to feed their children, feigning a lack of appetite themselves when supplies ran low. He saw it in glances exchanged between moms and dads as their progeny played and laughed and sang and squabbled.

Even fallen fathers loved their children, he knew, in the immoderate, extravagant way his Father loved him. Not as they might love a woman—with eddies of lust and pride and need and possession. Not as they loved work—a channel for their sweat and competence, a proclamation of self-sufficiency. They loved their children without reserve, without regard to future pain, without resistance or remorse. They loved them with a raw vulnerability that opened them to disappointment, rejection, and abandonment.

That's how his Father loved him. That's how his Father loved *them*.

So when it came time for him to speak of his Father's love, he reached for common ground, an image strong enough to carry the message of the Father's provision for all his wayward, rebellious children. "Which of you, if your son asks for bread, will give him a stone? Or if he asks for a fish, will give him a snake? If you, then, though you are evil, know how to give good gifts to your children, how much more will your Father in heaven give good gifts to those who ask him!" (Matt. 7:9–11).

He paused and watched a rough-hewn hand absently smooth a stubborn cowlick. He noticed a woman—caught by his words—passing another crust of bread to her fidgeting charges. He saw their heads nodding, these guardians of the future, agreeing they wanted to give good gifts to their sons and daughters . . . marveling that good gifts were what their Heavenly Father wanted to give them.

Yet he knew that, in spite of their love, most of these parents would fail to give good gifts to their children. Most of them—in years to come—would offer stones for bread, snakes for fish, baubles instead of principles, trinkets for truths. He knew—in spite of themselves, because they were broken—many of these fathers and mothers would leave their much-loved children only an accumulation of things that rusted and wore out rather than a legacy thieves could not steal and time could not corrode.

And he knew, with a confidence deep in his spirit, that his loving Father would never make that mistake with him . . . that his Father would never want other fathers and mothers to make that mistake with the future entrusted to them.[1]

Bread or Stone?

All of us want our lives to matter. We want who we are, what we have done, what we leave behind to make a difference in this world and for those we love.

Psychologists say it is not death we fear so much. It is *insignificance*—the idea that, at the end of the day, our lives didn't amount to all that much. That we didn't set ripples in motion to benefit the lives of our families and friends and world. That we failed to pass on our hard-won wisdom and cherished values and highest hopes to generations yet to come.

Most of us want to leave behind a financial blessing for the people we care about when we die. We have an instinctive desire to provide materially for our families after we're gone. Yet, at some deeper level, this desire extends far beyond the merely material. We long to share our dreams, our priorities, the principles by which we lived, and the values that fueled our efforts with the people we touched (and who touched us) on life's journey.

We know that, if we are to pass on more than our possessions, we cannot depend on the reading of a will to accomplish the task. We need to do something *now*—while we still have breath and health, when we can still touch and speak and shape—if we hope to share something more precious than assets.

Yet most of us have no intentional plan for doing this. We cannot put into words (clearly and succinctly) the values that form the core of our family. We can barely bring ourselves to talk about *money* with our heirs, much less the more difficult subjects of *expectations*, *priorities*, and *faith*. While some of us make detailed plans for passing on our wealth when we die, most of us have no similar plans *while we live* to prepare our heirs to use that wealth wisely . . . in a way that promotes family and faith priorities rather than merely a standard of living. We have no conversations mapped out, no stories we are determined to tell, that would clarify where our family came from, how we got here, the values that have shaped and sustained us, and the future we envision.

We rely instead on a mix of modeling, osmosis, side comments, and wishful thinking—hoping that, in the absence of a plan, the ones we leave behind might still absorb the best things we have to offer them and build their lives and futures on the same foundations that have grounded our own. We leave the most important mission of our lives—to pass something of consequence to the future—to chance or (as we say to comfort ourselves) "God's will."

We want our lives to mean something, to know that in our passage through this world we made a difference. But the truest measure of a life is not what is accomplished *during* life but the *ripples* a life sets in motion for the future and in those who are left behind. So ask yourself: Are you really willing to trust the measure of your life to unspoken hopes and unintended outcomes?

A Cautionary Tale

When the founder of one of America's largest frozen foods companies died in the mid-1990s, a fortune estimated at over five hundred million dollars was to be distributed among a small group of heirs: his second wife, their three children, his brother, and a cousin.

He had been meticulous in the management of his business affairs, running his company with an eye to every detail. His work life was a model of precision and efficiency. He was up at five o'clock for a one-hour swim, followed by breakfast at the club, then a staff meeting at eight o'clock sharp. Every minute of his day was focused and productive: reports, supplies, equipment, staffing.

He managed his personal life in much the same fashion. In fact, the only blip in his seventy-seven-year history was his divorce from a first wife when he was thirty-five. He and his second wife raised three children, served in their church, and supported local charities with generous enthusiasm.

He planned for the end of his life with the same careful precision. A team of seasoned CPAs, investment managers, and attorneys crafted a state-of-the-art plan that took several years to complete. The result was an impressive stack of contracts, agreements, trust documents, and inheritance instruments. He kept a copy in his office—three thick binders that mapped out what would happen to his wealth when he reached the end. It was a matter of pride with him (he lingered over the binders on occasion) that, immediately following his death, his estate would be settled seamlessly, and with great efficiency.

And then the frozen food king died.

Within hours, attorneys representing just about everybody the magnate had ever brushed against in life were filing briefs in the county courthouse. Stays. Writs. Pleadings. Injunctions. His three-volume estate plan was pronounced dead soon after he was.

His first wife, whom he'd not seen or talked with in over forty years, wanted *something.* The oldest son wanted *everything.* The middle son wanted *more.* The daughter's husband (no doubt deep in grief over the loss of his father-in-law) decided they should hold off on their own divorce proceedings and, instead, convinced his wife that she deserved a role in managing the company. The cousin claimed he helped invent the company's flash-freezing system but had never been adequately compensated. The brother decided years on the loading docks equipped him for a spot in the head office.

As for the grieving widow, her instructions to the phalanx of lawyers was simple: "To hell with them all. None of them deserves a dime." The legal wrangling still goes on. Several millions of dollars have been spent (so far) on legal and accounting fees. The traditional Christmas gathering around the parents' table has been on hold for years. And none of the kids is talking to mom—let alone to one another.

This competent, careful, conscientious man wanted to leave a mark on the future. But the mark he intended was not the mark he made. His business was carved up. His fortune was squandered. His family was destroyed.

He hoped to give bread and fish to his loved ones. But what he left them were stones and snakes.

The Measure of Life

The truest measure of your life is not what you accomplished, how much you amassed, how many "toys" you accumulated, what mistakes you made or avoided. Nothing you have done *during* your life is as important in determining your ultimate significance as what your loved ones do with you and yours *after* your life is over.

It is the mark you make on others, the mark you leave behind in the characters and commitments of those you love best, that will determine whether or not your life has made a difference. Grand achievements, great affluence, and good causes lose their luster if they remain *yours* . . . if they die with you. Real significance lies in equipping those you love to achieve greater things than you, to generate and use "treasures" more wisely than you, to give themselves to worthy causes more completely than you.

True, your children and friends will choose their own paths. You cannot control or manipulate the lives they will lead. Nothing you do can guarantee that those you love will make choices of which you would be proud. In spite of your best efforts and most careful planning and healthy relationships, you could lose everything you hoped for within years (sometimes within *days*) of your death.

That's not the point. God himself allows his children to make bad choices . . . to turn away, run away, stay away. He will not control or manipulate them to better lives. He will not protect them from the consequences of their own decisions. Even God has no guarantees where the future of his children is concerned.

But that doesn't keep God from *trying*.

Scripture is one long testimonial to a God who intentionally plans for the best future of his children. He expresses (clearly, if not succinctly!) the values that form the core of his family. He talks plainly about his principles and priorities—the principles and priorities he longs for his children to embrace. He holds conversations, he tells stories, he teaches life lessons. He discusses where we came from, why we are here, what ideals should shape and sustain us, the future he envisions for us. He explicitly lays out his expectations. He is unembarrassed to talk bluntly about treasure . . . both the worldly and the otherworldly kind.

While God will not compel the future we choose, he intends to influence and shape and inspire that future. When it comes to his plans and hopes and desires for us, in the effort to communicate them and urge us to choose the path of "life and prosperity" rather than the way of "death and destruction" (Deut. 30:15), God leaves nothing to chance or intuition or unspoken assumptions.

Can we do less?

Passing On a Legacy

Most parents want the best for their children. They honestly, sincerely want to give their children bread and fish, not stones and snakes. But what parents *want* and what too often *happens* are different things entirely.

Our experience (and a bulky body of evidence) indicates the likelihood is that what you really want to leave your family won't be anything like what they actually receive. They will not benefit from what you hoped for them or what you planned for them with your will and other legal documents. In the vast majority of cases, the things your family truly needs to thrive and prosper across the years won't even be discussed during your estate planning process.

That's because traditional estate (or death) planning focuses on material assets. It is managed by lawyers and accountants whose primary mission is transferring the greatest amount of assets with the smallest tax liability possible to eager heirs. Too many of these plans disintegrate the moment the assets begin to flow through the fingers of unprepared inheritors. Families battle over money. Children waste their inheritance in ways never envisioned (and certainly never encouraged) by their parents. Relationships disintegrate. Lives unravel. Wealth is frittered away. Healthy traditions are abandoned.

This is not, by any means, a criticism of the financial advisors who construct estate plans. They are doing the job (honestly and carefully) they have been retained to do. The responsibility of the traditional advisor is to transfer assets and reduce tax exposure, not to save families.

It is *your* job to protect your family, to ensure the people you leave behind realize that the most important asset you give them has nothing to do with money. It is a legacy larger than dollars and cents. It is a gift of family and faith and values and priorities. It is an attitude about living, not simply the means to sustain a standard of living.

Parents who plan for passing on only their material assets to their children, but don't plan for passing on the values and principles by which they lived, end up giving their children stones and snakes. Plans that place family valuables ahead of family values end up wasting both.

There are planning processes that help people put their families before their fortunes, increasing the likelihood that the family can thrive relationally and still prosper materially. Families who go through such processes come to a better understanding of their relationship to wealth and to one another. They learn to communicate more clearly and more honestly about things like money, philanthropy, and shared goals and objectives. They learn to see money as a tool to achieve the most important goals of all—family unity, individual achievement, and investment in matters that matter. They listen to stories about the hardships and triumphs that brought the family to where it is today, and they talk openly and from the heart about deeply important matters—like the sustaining quality of faith.

That's what this book is about: plans and processes focused on your legacy, helping you identify and talk about that legacy with your heirs, and moving you beyond wills and legal documents to a discussion of the things that matter most to you and are most important for the health and happiness of those you leave behind.

This is a book about giving good gifts—the best gifts—to your children. So what will it be for you and your family? Bread or stones?

Exercises

1. Are your essential "end of life" documents in place?
2. Is your will up-to-date and signed?
3. Have you determined "power of attorney"?
4. Do you have a "living will" (a directive to physicians about final care)?
5. If you have minor children, have you determined guardianship?
6. Do you plan to set up "trusts" for your heirs? Have you done so?
7. Does your executor/executrix know where to find important documents when needed?

Notes

1. This teaching was part of Jesus' Sermon on the Mount. See Matthew 7:9–11.

CHAPTER TWO

THE NINETY PERCENT RULE

The Challenge of Legacy

For years, the father planned to pass the estate to his sons.

House and barn. Fields and flocks. Servants and livestock and equipment. All of it for them. All of it for the two people he loved best in the world.

Still, the younger son's request caught him by surprise. "Father, give me my share of the estate . . . now."

It wasn't supposed to work that way. The "estate" was more than coins and accounts. This land was where the boys were born. They had all poured blood and sweat into those fields. They had given blistered hands and aching backs to the vineyards and orchards. The "estate" was where the boys had learned to work, to work together, to work for something larger than themselves. The "estate" meant immeasurably more than its monetary value.

And to ask for the inheritance while the father still lived! To reduce the father's lifework to nothing more than a purse of silver and gold! To walk away from family and future for the fickle promises of a far country! It broke the old man's heart. This wasn't how he meant to bless his son.

He did it anyway. Swallowing tears and disappointment, he put the coins in the hands of his youngest and watched him pack his bags for distant destinations. He didn't know whether the boy would be wise or foolish with the gift he'd been given. He didn't know if he would ever see the boy again. All he could do was wave a brave goodbye and watch the back of his son disappear down the road.

When the boy returned—broken and bowed—the father was glad to see him. It didn't matter that the money was gone. Didn't matter that the inheritance was squandered. His lost boy had been found. His dead son was alive to him once more. In a fit of celebration, the father killed the fatted calf.

Still, the older son's reaction caught him by surprise. Anger. Resentment. "I'm the good son, but you never celebrated me! He's the whoremonger, the wastrel, and he gets the party! I'm not coming in. I'm not welcoming him home."

It wasn't supposed to work that way. The two of them were brothers. They were meant to mean more to each other than that. What good were lands and buildings and crops without goodwill and peace and forgiveness? All those years. All that work. One son a failed pauper. And the other son a seething sea of bitterness and rage.

Alone, the father walked back to the house with the taste of ashes on his tongue.[1]

When Your Plans Backfire

Every parent wants to pass something on to their children, something to make better, more comfortable lives for their heirs. At the most obvious level, what we pass on involves material assets—money, a business, property, investments. To formalize the process of transferring those assets from one generation to another, most of us engage in some level of estate planning.

Estate planning can be as simple as what my grandmother did—stick tape to every piece of furniture in the house with the name of the intended recipient written upon it. She was poor, however, and had little in the way of worldly goods to pass along.

As the size of the estate grows, something more sophisticated is required. An estate plan worthy of the name is an intentional, purposeful, and detailed preparation for handing off wealth to the next generation. It involves several components:

- An enumeration and assessment of the assets in question.
- Naming the heirs.
- Specifying the terms of inheritance (who gets what, when, and how).
- Constructing a plan for the distribution of assets to heirs that minimizes federal and state taxes.

The net objective of most traditional estate planning has been to generate plans that will get as many goodies as possible out of the deceased's estate, past the IRS, and into the anxious embrace of waiting family members. Under this simple system, success is measured at the time the checks are written to the inheritors. Estate planning ends with the distribution of assets.

But what happens the next day? What happens to family health and happiness? What happens to relationships and traditions and family priorities? How do the heirs handle their inheritance? Well . . . such matters have not been the financial advisor's concern. So long as the estate is properly and legally distributed, the advisor has done his job.

Apply this measure of "successful" estate planning to the story that opens this chapter.

The father had a rather large estate, the fruit and reward of a lifetime's work. He knew what that estate was worth and could convert the value of his assets into coin. He knew who his heirs would be (his sons). He intended, planned, and specified that everything he owned pass to his boys.

The father had done all that was required by a good estate plan.

And the plan failed.

Don't get me wrong. The plan did exactly what it was designed to do. The estate was divided equally. The boys got their inheritance.

But notice what happened *after*. The younger son left, wasting his inheritance in wine and women. When—finally—he returned, the boy was broke and broken. Meanwhile, the older brother hacked at weeds in the fields he now owned. But inside, he churned with resentments and anger. The brothers were alienated. The father was heartbroken.

You don't have to read much into the story to know that this estate plan resulted in something very different from what the father intended: disrespect from his sons, a complete breakdown of the relationship between the two brothers, and the waste of the inheritance itself.

It happens all the time.

A Sad Story

The architect came to his lawyer's office with an urgent request. His father had a terminal illness and only a few years to live. He had built an estate worth over twelve million dollars but had not completed his estate planning. The architect said his father and mother knew exactly how they wanted their estate to be distributed. They had five children—three daughters and two sons—plus eighteen grandchildren. They wanted to take care of them all.

The sons had been successful in business and were financially independent. So the parents provided for trusts that would be accessible when the boys retired.

The daughters were more challenging. They had each walked a rocky road: divorced, in debt, and financially strapped. To help out their daughters, the parents had already purchased homes for each of them, paid in full. In addition, the parents specified that a significant amount of their wealth would be transferred immediately to the girls when they passed on.

The elderly couple's wishes were clear. There were no complex legal or financial issues to slow the process, so their estate planning documents came together quickly. Instruments were developed to transfer sums to the daughters, and tax-favorable trusts were created that would be paid to the sons in the future. From a purely legal and financial standpoint, this estate plan was well-thought-out, carefully crafted, and competently managed. It was, in fact, a textbook application of the best traditional estate planning available.

And it didn't work.

Soon after, both parents died (within a week of each other). Their deaths triggered the terms of their will. As planned, the estate's assets were protected from the IRS and divided among the heirs. The children received the inheritance their parents had intended.

Two years later, the architect returned to his lawyer's office. The story he recounted was heartbreaking. His family was being torn apart. His three sisters were again in deep financial trouble. Each had spent her share of the inheritance. Every penny. All three homes, gifts from the parents, had been mortgaged to the hilt to finance unsustainable lifestyles.

Now, the architect said, the sisters were demanding that he and his brothers tap their own inheritance trusts to help them, because it was "what mom and dad would want them to do." But how could the sons do that? They knew that any money the sisters were given would quickly evaporate. Their spending had always been out of control. The family was in chaos. The siblings were hurt and angry and estranged. They barely spoke to each other and, when they did, the talk always revolved around money.

It took less than twenty-four months for the daughters to spend most of the assets the parents had worked fifty years to build. Worse, the family unity all parents wish for their children was shattered. In a very real sense, all of that money and all of those carefully crafted asset-transfer plans and tax-reduction strategies had been for nothing.

And yet, it wasn't the planning that had failed. It accomplished exactly what it was designed to do: transfer the greatest amount of assets with the smallest tax liability possible to the heirs.

The operation, to cite the old saw, was a complete success. Pity the patient died.

The Odds Are Against You

Here is a sobering statistic: in families where new wealth is created by one generation, the family fortune will be gone by the end of the second generation in seven out of ten cases. By the end of the third generation, nine out of ten families will be broke.

Think about that for a moment. Ninety percent of couples who pass on material possessions to their children will have grandchildren who end up with little to nothing.

It's not a modern problem or unique to American culture. Two thousand years ago, a Chinese scholar penned the adage *fu bu guo san dai.* (Wealth never survives three generations.) A proverb that captured the same idea in thirteenth century England was "Clogs to clogs in three generations." (Wood-soled shoes were the common footwear of manual laborers and the poor in England at the time. While someone might accumulate sufficient wealth to eventually afford expensive leather boots, the proverb insists, his offspring would be wearing clogs again soon.) English poet John Dryden put it this way: "Seldom three descents continue good."

Adam Smith summed it up over two hundred years ago in his landmark book *The Wealth of Nations*: "Riches, in spite of the most violent regulations of law to prevent their dissipation, very seldom remain long in the same family."

In the long run (sometimes in the short!), ninety percent of all inheritance plans will fail to accomplish what is so earnestly hoped and desired.

There is no other area of our lives where we would take such odds lying down. Imagine a world where there was a ninety percent probability that you'd take a tumble the minute you got out of bed. Then, a nine-out-of-ten chance that there would be no hot water when you stepped into the shower. A ninety percent likelihood that there would be no food in the refrigerator, that your car wouldn't start, that (if by some miracle it did) you'd suffer an accident once your car got on the road.

A ninety percent probability of anything happening makes that event, by statistical standards, an actuarial certainty.

And we wouldn't stand for it! We would insist that something had to change! We'd start studies and alter habits and enact laws. We'd initiate plans and take aggressive actions. We'd hold people responsible and drive ourselves relentlessly to discover a solution.

Except, apparently, when it comes to the financial future of our families. The Ninety Percent Rule has dominated families across cultures, over centuries, rich or poor. It is the norm when it comes to passing on material assets to children and grandchildren: ninety percent of families will fail to do this in a way that keeps those assets secure, growing, and available to the family.

And we accept those odds with barely a whimper or an objection. We don't show much alarm or even awareness. We make no plans beyond a basic will (and over half of Americans do not even have that!). We procrastinate and postpone and avoid. We hope against hope that everyone will live happily ever after when we are gone.

That's frightening. But consider an even more frightening possibility. The Ninety Percent Rule applies to the simplest, the most tangible, and the most quantifiable gift we leave to our families: money. It applies to an arena of life where many of us do at least *some* planning and give a *little* thought. It applies to a subject we can talk about clearly and candidly with our families (when we are pushed and prodded to do so by threat of lawyers or death).

What do you imagine the odds are for successfully passing on gifts that are more complicated, less concrete, and unquantifiable—like the importance of family harmony, the worth of the family name and reputation, the centrality of faith, or the values and traits and traditions that define who we are as a family? What are the probabilities of successfully handing off values, ideals, and principles when there is no particular plan for doing so? What are the chances that a family will continue to embrace and support aspirations and visions we cannot name, much less talk about in a frank and straightforward manner?

If the odds are stacked against passing on our valuables, how much less likely is it that we will pass on our values? If we fail ninety percent of the time in providing for our family's long-term financial future, what is the failure rate for providing a legacy that will keep our family healthy and happy, creative and productive, generous and faithful in the generations to come?

The money is the easy part. It's the *meaning* that's difficult. What good is it, really, to pass on possessions without passing on the ethics that produced them, the attitudes that managed them, or the priorities that determined how they were utilized? So what if your heirs inherit the world from you? If they lose their souls as a result, where's the profit in that?

Bad News/Good News

There is no way to sugarcoat it: a ninety percent failure rate is bad news.

There is good news, however, to be found in this frightening statistic. It's hidden in that other ten percent . . . those families who manage to pass on wealth and protect their family's health for longer than two generations. It wasn't luck that allowed these families to survive and thrive. There are specific habits and attitudes, motivations and strategies, that Ten Percent Families share in common.

Rodney Zeeb and Ryan Zeeb (with the Heritage Institute) address these "elements of success" in a white paper entitled "The Elements of Heritage Planning."[2] Based on experience, research, and interviews with families, they identified twelve characteristics and habits that are commonly found in families that beat the Ninety Percent Rule.

Ten Percent Families do the following:

1. Foster strong and effective communication and build trust between generations.
2. Develop, maintain, and regularly revisit a vision for the family's present and future.
3. Meet regularly.
4. Promote a balanced definition of the meaning of "wealth."
5. Keep the family business separate from the business of being a family.
6. Identify the roles necessary for the family to be successful (financially and otherwise).
7. Inspire individual family members to participate for their own individual reasons.
8. Train and mentor each generation.
9. Facilitate the genuine transfer of leadership from generation to generation.
10. Require true collaboration between professional advisors.
11. Create mechanisms for ongoing family governance.
12. Do it now.

They concluded: "For the successful 10%, achieving multi-generational unity and prosperity is not just the result of doing good financial and estate planning. Instead, lasting success comes about because they add an essential third element to their planning, one that has come to be known as heritage planning."[3]

This book is dedicated to helping you and your family beat the Ninety Percent Rule. By building on these twelve "elements of success" and helping readers understand a process for defining and transmitting family values and faith to future generations, we offer you practical tools for becoming a Ten Percent Family.

Does Faith Exempt You from the Ninety Percent Rule?

The easy thing to do when confronted with these frightening odds and tragic possibilities is to take refuge in your faith. "This won't happen to me. I go to church and pray and try to live a good life. The Ninety Percent Rule only applies to families that don't put God first."

Really? Then why—in Scripture—do so many "good" parents struggle to pass on a meaningful inheritance to their children?

Adam, no doubt, was the best father he could be. He had an entire world to bequeath to his sons. The outcome? One son murdered. The other, a wanderer without place and without peace.

Jacob was blessed by God, a wealthy man with flocks and herds and riches to pass on to his children. But all Jacob's wealth could not produce peace among his wives, or harmony between his sons, or protect his best-loved boy (Joseph) from years of suffering and struggle.

King David was not a perfect man. Still, he was known as a "man after God's own heart." He gave a throne to his son Solomon as an inheritance. But Solomon brought the kingdom to spiritual bankruptcy during his reign. And when *his* son, Rehoboam, became king, he lost half the kingdom in the first three days of his foolish governance.

The father in the story of the prodigal was not an evil man. No doubt he honored God and read the Torah and tithed to the temple. But devoutness did not inoculate this good father from raising difficult sons.

Some of the greatest heroes of the biblical story were not able to pass on a meaningful inheritance to their children. They loved God. They had the best intentions. But they never learned the secret of preparing an inheritance plan for their heirs that included preparing their heirs for the inheritance.

People of faith need to recognize that handing off a legacy is hard work. It requires planning and disciplined execution. It takes time and energy and prayer. Even then, the odds aren't good. Even faithful, loving, well-intentioned parents can fail the future.

We are convinced (and our experience confirms) that thoughtful planning can make a decisive difference in the way the future of a family unfolds. By expanding the concept of "planning" beyond the traditional focus on estates and possessions to include values and character, we can significantly increase the likelihood that our loved ones will receive the very best inheritance we have to offer—our valuables *and* our values.

We don't have to watch our children wander down the road to some far country. We don't have to witness the ones we love grow alienated and distant. Our families don't have to be another statistic in support of the Ninety Percent Rule.

We can write a different ending to our story. That different ending begins by asking four simple questions.

Exercises

1. Review and reread your will(s) out loud to your spouse, your executor, a trusted friend, or a counselor.
   - Do you understand the terms of your will?
   - Do those terms still reflect your desires?
   - Have you included the Kingdom of God in your testamentary planning?
2. Review your 401(k), IRAs, and life insurance policies for accurate beneficiary designations. Don't assume these documents are correct. Look!

Notes

1. Luke 15:11–32.

2. "Sustaining Family Wealth & Unity across Generations," *The Heritage Institute*, white paper, www.theheritageinstitute.com/Whitepaper.html. Request a copy (and self-assessment) by emailing www.theacufoundation.org.

3. Ibid.

CHAPTER THREE

FOUR QUESTIONS

Defining Your Legacy

Perhaps people are right when they say, "There is no such thing as a dumb question."

People say that. Jesus didn't.

"Which of us is the greatest?" is a question the disciples debated among themselves; Jesus just shook his head. Many of the questions put to him by the religious leaders seemed foolish to him: "Why don't your disciples fast?" "Should we pay taxes to Caesar?" "Why do you eat with tax collectors and sinners?" And some of the questions shouted by the crowds were just plain wrong-headed: "What sign will you show us?" "Will you give us bread?"

As difficult as some questions were for him, few things gave Jesus more joy than a really good question. The man kneeling in front of him had just asked a beauty.

"What must I do to inherit eternal life?"

It took a special person to ask such a great question . . . someone who was thinking ahead . . . someone who valued kingdom things. Jesus saw something exceptional in this man. Perhaps it was his posture: kneeling on the dusty road in submission and supplication. Perhaps it was a look in his eye, an innocent face unmarked by regrets or shame.

"You know the commandments," Jesus answered. "Do what God wants you to do."

"I've tried to do just that, Teacher," the man declared, "since I was a boy."

Jesus looked more closely and recognized a kindred spirit. He knew a spiritual man when he saw one. He knew this man wanted to do what was right. But Jesus—with his sharp eyes and uncanny ability to read the heart of others—knew more. The man before him was well-dressed. His hair and beard were carefully barbered. There were gold rings on his fingers. He had never known hunger.

"One more thing I ask of you," Jesus told the man tenderly. "Give away your possessions and come be my disciple."

The man's face fell. His shoulders slumped. He took a deep, gasping breath. And then he staggered to his feet and stumbled away without another word. For he was a wealthy man, grown accustomed to the privileges of prosperity. And Jesus had just asked him to do the one thing he could not, would not do—even to secure eternal life.

This man asked Jesus a good question. But it turns out he couldn't handle the answer.[1]

In Search of Good Questions

If you are determined to pass on a legacy, if you believe you have something more than money to give to those you love, then there are a few crucial questions you must ask . . . good questions that force you to think ahead . . . hard questions that probe and pry and push. It is important to ask good questions if you intend to convey a meaningful legacy.

There are four fundamental questions you should confront as you consider what remains of your life and the certainty of your death. The answers to these four questions map out a plan that can change the future.

Who are my heirs?

When you die, who will you leave behind? Who will be affected by your death because they have been so intimately connected to your life?

The easy answer to this first question (the answer that usually comes from thinking primarily in terms of a financial inheritance) is that your heirs are your spouse and children. Maybe a few members of your extended family. Those are the people to focus on, conventional wisdom suggests, as you think about and plan for your death.

In fact, the real answer is a little more complicated. You have built a network of relationships over the course of your life: family, certainly, but also friends and mentors, spiritual companions, neighbors and associates, people who labored with you on worthy and common causes. There are people who have blessed your life and to whom you have been a blessing. You would feel the absence of these people profoundly. You hope they will feel your absence when you are gone.

The first question you must answer in the quest to leave a legacy is not about *financial* dependents but, rather, about *relational* connections. Who do you love? Who loves you? Who has shaped you? Whom have you shaped? Who shares your priorities? Who has partnered with you in projects and passions? Whose lives have intertwined with yours? What causes have you adopted and championed?

If you stop (for a moment) defining your heirs *financially* and think (instead) of your relational heirs, the list of your "beneficiaries" grows exponentially. Your true heirs are not limited to those connected to you by marriage license or strands of DNA. Rather, they are the people who have been a blessing to you, the people you've had a chance to influence and shape, the people you've bumped into along the currents and eddies of your life. Your heirs are those who carry your genes *and* your mark, those who carry on your name *and* your mission. Who are the people who have made your life possible, productive, and pleasurable? Who has your life blessed and bettered? Make a list. Name the names. Identify the significant relationships you've accumulated over the years.

In Appendix B is a worksheet (*My Heirs,* 199) that will help you do this. By working through this "map" of your most meaningful relationships, by listing specific names and particular entities, you will come to recognize that you have more heirs than you realize. Not all of them will (or should) receive a financial bequest from you (as the next paragraphs will suggest). But you owe something to a wide variety of people who have nurtured you over the years, individuals and causes in whom you have invested.

What do I leave behind?

The second question you should ask in the quest to leave a legacy is about the legacy itself. What exactly do you want to leave to the people you love? What do you want others to "inherit" from you?

Again, the easy answer is to equate "inheritance" with material possessions . . . to think only of finances when you consider what you will give your heirs. A better answer is more complicated and nuanced. Yes, you want to pass on your money. But is that all? Is that the extent of the blessings you would bequeath to the future?

The rest of this book is devoted to helping you answer this question: "What do I leave behind?" As you read, you will realize that you are more (and have more to offer) than bank accounts and portfolios. The chapters to follow will grow and deepen your appreciation of your true legacy. It is this *legacy*, not just worldly goods, that defines your actual wealth.

At the start of this exploration, however, some preliminary thinking about what you offer the people you love is in order.

We've included a table (*My Gifts*, 201–202) in Appendix B to help you appreciate the diversity of wealth you can pass along to your loved ones. Spending a little time with the question "What do I leave behind?" will not only prepare you for the insights of the remainder of this book, but it will encourage you to recognize just how "rich" you really are.

As you think through these matters, you are actually taking the first and necessary steps toward defining your legacy. You're identifying the matters that matter most to you—the parts of yourself you want to leave to those who survive you. When you think about it, you'll probably discover that your financial bequest is not the most important contribution you want to pass to the future. It may not even be in your top five!

Asking this question leads you to realize that leaving an *estate* is not your highest priority. . . it's a greater and broader *legacy* that's the point. It's not simply the accumulation of your possessions you would pass along but the distillation of your character and commitments and deepest convictions.

Transferring portfolios and possessions to heirs should form *part* of your planning for the future. But it should not be the exclusive or dominant focus of your planning . . . you have more important gifts to give.

Once you stop defining your bequest to the future in exclusively financial terms and start seeing your gifts to the future in broader categories, the potential for blessing the important people in your life with more than money grows accordingly.

Another table (*Who Gets What from Me?*, 203) in Appendix B invites you to match your relationships with your gifts. Not everyone in your life gets (or needs) the same thing from you. You will feel a responsibility to take care of some people financially (e.g., your spouse and children, a favorite charity, the entities that perpetuate what you value most). Others, however, should be thanked or blessed or verbally affirmed or granted a bit of wisdom or presented with a memento. You'll want some of your heirs to inherit every category of "gift" you have to give. Some will (and should) receive a more limited inheritance from you. As you think about your true heirs, think also about what you will pass on to each of them.

By all means, plan and specify your *financial* bequests. But recognize there are other kinds of gifts you can bestow that cost you little (when measured in material terms). You can say "thanks." You can acknowledge influences. You can affirm character. You can offer forgiveness and ask for the same. You can speak words of praise and commendation and respect. (Most of the people around us are deserts, thirsty to drink the life-giving water of our verbal blessing.) You can recommend good habits and good people. You can bear testimony to the importance of faith in your life. You can enunciate the philosophy that has been your guide and shelter. You can list the lessons life has taught you (often by pointing to the scars you've accumulated along the way). You can tell your story and the story of your family. You can confess your faults. You can speak to the joys of books and music and fly-fishing.

The encouragement, support, and release such gifts provide cost little, but they are worth a great deal to the people you love. You have the power to give these gifts so long as you live. If these gifts are withheld, however, they can never be granted once you are gone. And your heirs will be impoverished as a result.

How will I pass on my legacy?

The third question you should ask in the quest to leave a legacy is *how* you will accomplish this task. By what means and methods will you place the best of yourself in the hands of your heirs? And, as important, how do you plan to prepare your heirs to receive, benefit from, and bless others with the inheritance you pass along?

If passing on your valuables were your only priority, all you would really need is a legal will: a listing of assets, a designation of who gets what. But if passing on your *legacy* is the point, a piece of paper is not sufficient. Everybody leaves "stuff" behind. Not everyone communicates a larger legacy.

You can hope that a legacy "transfer" will happen fortuitously, without thought or intent, without process or strategy. You might excuse a lack of planning by believing you are better off just "letting things happen" and "taking a hands-off approach." (By the way, if you really buy that, I have some oceanfront property in Arizona I'd like to sell you.)

Yet everything we've learned in life teaches us the opposite. Good things rarely result from lack of vision and planning. It's hard to hit the bull's-eye when you don't aim at a target. It's more likely that, without a plan, the hand-off of our future will be fumbled and bumbled, our inheritance mishandled and botched, our hopes turned to dust.

Do you have such a plan? Are there steps you intend to take, stories you mean to tell, conversations about "matters that matter" you want to have with the people you love best?

A plan for passing along your legacy is different from a plan for passing along your assets. Traditional estate planning—focused on investments and trusts, spreadsheets and valuations, bank accounts and property, and financial and legal instruments—is, and always will be, the necessary vehicle for the transmission of *things*. But wills and spreadsheets can never convey the values, the traditions, the faith, and the traits that have shaped your unique family history for many years.

More powerful tools, more robust processes will be required if you want to pass on something of greater value than your valuables. Much of what follows in this book goes into greater detail about these plans and processes, and makes practical suggestions about *how* you can effectively transmit your legacy to your loved ones.

But a good place to begin is by considering the tools you'll be working with.

Most of us are aptly described by the old adage, "To a man who has only a hammer, everything looks like a nail." When it comes to preparing for death, many reach for one primary tool: a legal will. But even the brief description of legacy just given should convince you of the inadequacy of this one tool for passing along every gift.

The *My Tools* table (204–205) in Appendix B can help you think more specifically about the broad toolset available for different legacy tasks. Not every tool is adequate for every job. A compliment might be a great tool for affirming and encouraging someone you love. You need that tool in your toolbox. But compliments are lousy tools for specifying how your material assets are to be distributed. Every legacy task has an appropriate and effective tool. The table we've included invites you to consider which tools might be most suitable and helpful in transmitting different aspects of your legacy.

The number and variety of tools available are overwhelming—once we begin thinking about how we pass on more than our money. What family stories do you need to tell in order to underscore the importance of certain principles or character traits? What biblical or autobiographical stories should become the "stuff of legend" in your relational circles—stories so frequently told that they lodge in the memories of family and friends, shaping their goals and ideals? Who are your heroes? Why are these people heroes in your mind? Do others know what these heroes mean to you and how they made a difference in your life? Make a list of your ten favorite books . . . your five favorite sayings . . . your three guiding principles. Write out your faith testimony and your personal mission statement.

In later chapters, we will talk about creating opportunities for telling stories and sharing personal facts and favorite memories. Sharing such stories and testimonials with loved ones is as important as figuring out what stocks and bonds you want to share. For the moment, however, recognize that every task has its tool and every tool has its use. If you want to pass a house or bank account to your heirs, a will (or other legal document) is the perfect tool to accomplish that. But if you want to pass along your faith, or a particular character trait, or a way of treating people, there are other tools better suited to the task. Your challenge, at this point, is to enlarge your collection of tools, understand the purposes for which they are best suited, and develop your skills in using them.

Why do I want to leave a legacy?

The final question to struggle with in the quest to leave a legacy is "Why?" Why bother worrying about the future? You'll be gone! Why spend any of the life still remaining to plan for the death that awaits you? Frankly, the subject is a bit morbid . . . and not a little depressing!

So why think about it? Depending on your motivation, you won't . . . or you will, but for the wrong reasons . . . or you will because there are people and causes and ideas that you'll care about even when you're past caring.

Here are a few people who won't be motivated to think about their legacy:

- People who face their deaths just as they have lived their lives: selfishly, without regard for the good of others, intent on their own personal needs. They won't think about the future simply because they won't be around to enjoy it.
- People who are convinced they have little to offer their heirs because of personal struggles and failings. Some people may be *afraid* to think of the future, with more reasons to evade or deny what they leave behind than to find that one "rose" they could pass along.
- Tragically, people who have no financial inheritance to offer their heirs. They might believe, as a consequence, that they have no legacy to leave. They do not recognize the other "treasures"—hard work, honesty, kindness, joy, faith—they can offer in money's stead. Or, at least, they won't give the thought and planning to passing those things on that they would to things of monetary value.

I believe better things of you and your motives, dear reader. You are the kind of person willing to think long and hard about tomorrow, even when you might not make it to tomorrow yourself. You're not protecting yourself or your image or even your achievements. You are thinking about the future because there are people you love and wish the best for . . . there are causes that are worthy and making a difference . . . and there are ideas and ideals that you believe to be foundational to any healthy, meaningful life.

Those are good reasons for thinking about the future, for planning to pass on a legacy: for the sake of the people you love, on behalf of the causes you support, and in service of the values you believe in.

Once again, we have included a table (*My Motives*, 205) in Appendix B, listing some possible motivations for leaving a legacy. I'm certainly not recommending every motive on the list. But you need to give careful and honest consideration to *why* you care about what happens after you are gone—even if those reasons are not very pretty. Knowing your "why" will help you answer questions about "who" and "what" and "how." So even if you have to confess to some less-than-stellar motives (or, as is true of us all, a mess of mixed motives), clarity about your reasons will lead to clarity about your legacy.

Conclusion

When it comes to thinking about the future—how you want to conclude your life and the legacy you intend to leave—there are some good questions to ask. While it may be true that there are no dumb questions, it is foolish not to ask these particular questions of yourself as you face the reality of your family's future.

So take the time, do the work, of asking some basic questions about what happens . . . after *you*. But understand that, as hard as the questions are, *asking* is the easy part.

Why ask questions if you can't handle the answers? Why ask at all if you can't muster the courage to do something meaningful with your answers?

Many people don't have what it takes even to ask. Fewer still are willing to face the answers and embrace the implications.

So, what kind of person are you?

Exercises

There are a series of exercises included in Appendix B. These worksheets can help you think through your gifts, heirs, tools, and motives. Here are a few samples:

- Name one emotional characteristic you possess that you would like to give your heirs (e.g., joy, stability, fearlessness, maturity).
- Who have been your significant mentors or teachers?
- What are your core family stories?
- I've learned there are values and character traits that lead to a happier life, and I would like to give those to my kids.

Note

1. Mark 10:17–23.

CHAPTER FOUR

BUILDING YOUR TOWER

An Intentional Legacy

"I want to change my whole life," the man with a hard-lived face told him.

"Do you?" Jesus asked him, smiling.

"I'll become your disciple, Master. The best follower you've ever known!" shouted another, dressed in rags and leaning on a crutch.

"Will you?" Jesus called back.

"I'll give up everything for you," said a third—a woman with the glow of the zealot in her eyes.

"Really?" asked Jesus.

He looked around at the people pressing on him, making their promises, offering their futures. "Let me tell you a story."

His listeners grew still, faces fixed on his. They loved his stories.

"Once there was a man who decided to build a tower. He wanted a tower badly. He went right out and started to dig the foundations. He dug and he dug. The sun climbed higher in the sky as he dug, getting hotter as the day progressed. The man sweat buckets. His strength and his enthusiasm began to wane by the afternoon. He sat on a pile of dirt to rest.

"Looking at all his hard work, the man suddenly realized he didn't have the money to build a tower. He couldn't afford the bricks and mortar, the wood for a door, the shingles for a roof. He threw his shovel down in disgust and walked away. What would you think about such a man?"

"A foolish man, I'd call him," a wizened woman near the front of the crowd answered. "He wanted something, but he gave no thought to getting it! He had no plan!" She tipped her head and spat on the ground, a measure of her disdain for such people.

"Good," Jesus agreed. "Once there was a king who wanted to make war. He didn't count his soldiers, he didn't study his enemy. He just sounded the trumpets and marched his armies into the unknown. When, finally, he realized he was badly outnumbered, the only thing he could do was beg his enemy for terms of peace. He lost without even fighting. What would you think about such a king?"

"A foolish king!" the same woman answered. "No thought again! No plan! Off with his head!"

Jesus smiled. "Quite right." And then the smile faded and his eyes pierced the people surrounding him. "We want all sorts of things, don't we? Towers and battles. Different lives. A different future. But *wanting* something isn't enough, my friends. Unless you know the cost and can pay the price, unless you think and plan and sacrifice, wishes remain only wishes. You can never build a tower, or a life, on good intentions and fervent hopes. Do you understand?"

The people around him avoided his eyes. They looked at the ground, at their hands, at the clouds scudding across the summer skies. Anywhere but at him.

"Now," said Jesus, smiling again. "There is a cost to being my disciple. Which of you is willing to pay it?"[1]

Good Intentions? Or Intentionality?

In 2005, the Allianz Life Insurance Company surveyed baby boomers and their parents on a wide range of family and finance related issues. "Many people wrongly assume that the most important issue among families is money and wealth transfer. It's not," said Dr. Ken Dychtwald, the survey designer. "Non-financial items that parents leave behind—like ethics, morals, faith, and religion—are ten times more important to both boomers and their parents than the financial aspects of inheritance. In fact, seventy-seven percent of those surveyed (age forty plus) said the most important inheritance they could receive or pass on would be values and lessons about life."[2]

Despite that overwhelming sentiment, the survey also reported that fewer than one-third of those responding had actually *done* anything about translating those wishes into action. No intentional conversations between parents and children, no purposeful family meetings, and no formal documents. Lots of people *want* to leave a legacy. Not many of them, however, count the cost and pay the price of doing so.

That sad fact shouldn't be surprising. In all probability, you are among the unprepared majority. Not because you *want* to be unprepared. Not because you don't care about passing on a larger legacy to your family. Simply, rather, because you have not taken the time and invested the effort to translate your wishes into reality. There is a cost to handing on the future to those you love. Most people haven't counted that cost, or—if they have—they can't bring themselves to pay it.

Don't believe me? Appendix C (*Legacy Planning Assessment*, 208–210) is an assessment designed to help you determine your level of preparedness for handing off both your valuables and your values to your heirs. This exercise asks you to rate (on a scale of 1 to 5) the progress you have made in communicating a legacy to your heirs . . . and in preparing your heirs to receive that legacy.

It will ask about relatively simple inheritance matters (the development of wills, identity of executors, and awareness of your estate plans on the part of your heirs). But it will also ask about more complicated issues. About conversations you need to have with the people you love on subjects ranging from faith to friendship to philosophy of life. About stories you should tell about your heritage and your journey. About your long-term hopes and plans for the health and peace of your family.

Are you building your tower, or are you just wishing you would? Have you started yet? Have you made a good beginning but recognize there is a long way to go? Can you step back from your family's future and see, with confidence, that you have done everything in your power to build a future that has a strong foundation, sturdy pillars and beams, and a roof to shelter your heirs from storms to come?

You might want to turn to the *Legacy Planning Assessment* (208–210) right now and spend a few moments answering some critical questions about your legacy and your family. Questions like:

- Have you clarified long-term plans and hopes (i.e., legacy) for your family beyond the distribution of financial assets?
- Have you written a family vision statement?
- Have you identified the family traditions you hold dear and hope will continue?

When you come back, enter your *average score* here: _____. Your results may shock you, discourage you, overwhelm you.

That's okay. In some ways, the assessment is *meant* to be shocking. It is intended to help you count the cost of legacy and determine whether that is a cost you are willing to pay. What is important at the moment is not where you *are* with these matters but where you will *go*, not what you *wish* were true but what you intend to *do* about it.

The majority of people—when confronted with questions like these—discover they are not where they want to be in building a future for their families. Good intentions. High hopes. But vague directions and poor tools and feeble execution.

What we need is a plan!

Intentional Planning

Like the tower-builder and the warrior-king whose stories began this chapter, our greatest hurdles are not our intentions but our intentionality.

Each of them had a goal and was motivated to reach that goal. But between desire and execution, there were some hard realities they should have faced. What materials were required? What resources were needed? How should they proceed? What were their chances of success?

These two men were in desperate need of a good plan. A good plan would have convinced them that preparations were necessary—saving some money, for instance, or spying on the opponent. A good plan would have focused them on *logistics*—the "who, what, where, when, and how" that are so necessary to successful projects. A good plan might have persuaded them not to pull the trigger before they loaded the gun (if you'll forgive the anachronism).

So . . . do you have a plan for defining your true legacy and then transmitting it to your heirs?

Making a plan (moving from intention to intentionality) will require us to stop wishing and hoping and start preparing. To do *that* will mean we give up on the illusion that our heirs will soak up our values by osmosis and commit ourselves, instead, to adopting intentional strategies, to developing specific habits, and to sharing family values in effective ways.

The purpose of this book is to help you make good progress toward passing on your greatest legacy to the people you love most. In the chapters that follow, we will be looking at plans, strategies, and tools for conveying that legacy.

But you don't have to read the entire book in order to develop an initial strategy. So, here is a brief checklist to consider as you think about building your legacy tower.

- ❑ Turn down the corner of this page. (You'll be coming back to this list repeatedly.)
- ❑ Read the first four chapters of this book. (Hopefully, you can check this one off!)
- ❑ Do the exercises in Appendix B (*My Heirs, My Gifts,* etc.).
- ❑ Do the *Legacy Planning Assessment* included in Appendix C.
- ❑ Make room in your schedule for prayer, reflection, and planning.
- ❑ Pray.
- ❑ Consider carefully whether you need a *facilitator* to help you navigate toward legacy.
- ❑ Write a letter to your great-great-grandchildren.
- ❑ Do the hard work of "Guided Discovery" (see Chapter Seven).

❑ Write a "Family Vision Statement" (see Chapter Eight).
❑ Pray and plan for an initial retreat with your family (see Chapter Nine).
❑ Hold an initial "Family Retreat" with your family (see Chapter Ten).
❑ Make plans for ongoing, annual retreats to build on the legacy foundations you are pouring.

Important Steps in Your Plan

Many of the items in the list are covered in other chapters of this book. But a few, while obvious, bear some initial examination. As you prepare to build your legacy tower, consider the importance of the following tasks.

Making Room in Your Schedule

Stephen Covey comments on something very basic but very essential to intentional planning: "The key is not to prioritize what's on your schedule, but to schedule your priorities."[3]

Everyone is busy. All of us are hounded and harassed by the demands of our calendars. Every moment of every day seems gobbled up by urgent matters, other people's emergencies, the details and detritus of living life and doing business and juggling commitments.

"Busyness" is the characteristic disease of modern life.

But few of us *die* from that disease. What kills us is the absence of *significance* in our schedules . . . not how crammed our hours are but how little the activities in those hours reflect our deepest priorities.

If passing on a legacy to your loved ones is important to you, you have to commit the necessary time. Room for prayer and reflection and writing. Space for asking good questions and sifting through the rich ore of your own heart. You don't need to set aside weeks and months at a stretch. You may only be able to devote a couple of hours a week . . . a few moments each day.

But you cannot build a legacy without paying a price in time.

So make a date with yourself (daily? weekly?) for the sake of your family's future. Give yourself regular "pauses" in your hectic schedule to do something that is truly important.

Making a Commitment to Prayer

If you haven't recognized your need for divine intervention by now, a few words in a book won't make a difference. But when I am bumping up against matters of profound importance, significant impact, and highest hopes, I need help. Not the kind that comes from best-selling books or the well-intended advice of friends. Heavenly help. Sacred support.

I pray.

You pray for your family on a regular basis. You probably pray for your children, by name, whenever you speak to God. But have you prayed about your legacy? Here is a brief prayer outline to use as you converse with God about your family's future.

- Grant blessings and protection for my family and heirs.
- Allow me to give my children bread and fish, not stones or snakes.
- Don't let my family fall victim to the Ninety Percent Rule.
- Help me remember that preparing my heirs to receive their inheritance is more important than the size of the inheritance they receive.
- Grant me wisdom to recognize my true legacy.
- Grant me discipline to finish the legacy tower I'm trying to build.
- Help me not to mistake good intentions with intentionality.

It won't take you long to pray this legacy prayer. But praying it daily will keep you focused and humble and eager for God's help.

Finding a Partner on the Journey

You've already realized that defining and transmitting your legacy is not a simple or short process. It requires dialogue and discernment, devotion and discipline.

A little expertise and experience can't hurt.

If you're going to build a tower, some construction skills are needed. If you intend to lead an army, some military know-how helps.

One of the most important decisions you will make about the legacy process (important for doing it right, important to finishing what you start) is whether to invite a competent, experienced partner to join you on the journey.

There are people who have made this journey before, people who specialize in the quest for legacy. They have the training, skills, and track record to assist you toward your goal. They can help you build your legacy tower. At the end of this book are recommended *facilitators* (236–238), ready, willing, and competent to guide you and your family on this adventure.

You can make this journey on your own. (This book is designed to help you self-navigate the legacy road.) But nothing makes the trip go smoother than a partner who has "been there, done that" and knows the way.

Writing a Letter to Posterity

"Begin with the end in mind" is another Stephen Covey jewel.

As you think about legacy, the "end" is not what you have accomplished in life or what happens on the day of your death. It's not even how your children are impacted by the legacy they inherit. It's about their children . . . and their children's children. It's about the long-term health and happiness of your descendents, the generations yet unborn.

If you want to "begin with the end in mind," start by writing a letter to your great-great-grandchildren.

The purpose of this letter is to "pass a torch" to them. The torch is you. Think about what was meaningful in your life, what you did that was good, what you wish you could have changed, what you hope for them.

Dear Great-Great-Granddaughter (or Grandson),

We've never met. But I love you and want you to know that I was thinking about you long before you were born. You are part of my family.

A long time ago, I tried to pass along a family legacy that I hope is still intact and still a blessing. Nothing would please me more than to know you have heard the story of our family . . . that you understand what is important in life, what is really valuable . . . that you have inherited not only some material things from your parents but also some of the principles and faith that make life worth living.

Then introduce yourself. Take a paragraph to tell the basics of your life. When and where you lived. What was most important to you. Why your life mattered.

And then pass your legacy to them. Include a copy of your Family Vision Statement (which you will write in Chapter Eight). Make photocopies of your notes for the exercises in this book (especially those at the end of Chapter Three and Chapter Seven). Enclose a photograph of yourself and your present family. Include a copy of your Family Tree.

Close the letter with a word of blessing. Something like:

> I wish you joy and peace and meaning and love. May you taste
> all the good things in life. May you discover the power of faith
> and purpose and ministry and friendship. Remember . . . a long
> time ago, I reached out to you with a legacy. My greatest prayer is
> that you have been touched by that legacy and that it has been a
> blessing in your life.

Now, take out a large envelope, include the letter and the other documents, seal it, and then write "To my great-great-grandchild" on the front. Put it in a safe place alongside the other significant papers you want your descendents to inherit. Add a handwritten codicil to your will requesting that the "letter" be kept safe and, eventually, delivered to your distant offspring.

Writing this letter will not be an easy task. But what a rare opportunity: to speak from the grave and talk to your great-great-granddaughter! Imagine her reading your letter eagerly, soaking in what you write, and responding with, "I've heard stories about _____! A family hero! That's the person who defined what it means to be a [family surname]!" What a rush! What a thrill! What a sense of accomplishment! And what a validation of the steps you are taking in the present to prepare your family in the future.

Counting the Cost of Legacy

The idea of legacy lies at the heart of this book. Understanding what a legacy is and how you can build a lasting legacy that will benefit your family for generations to come—that's where our conversation is headed.

But first, you need to count the cost. *Wanting* to pass on a legacy is not enough. The best of intentions are not sufficient. You can't even do something simple (like build a tower) without resources and a plan. How much harder is it to do something profound (like place your legacy into the hands of your heirs) without thinking through how to get from wishes to completion!

Only you can determine what you will do with this legacy challenge. There are those who never even begin. There are those (like the characters in the parable) who start but can't finish. And then there are those who, once they've started, have the fortitude to finish strong. May their tribe increase. May you be counted among their number.

Exercises

The *Legacy Planning Assessment* can be found in Appendix C. It includes a worksheet to help you assess how well prepared you (and your heirs) are for passing along (and receiving) a legacy, not just an inheritance.

Notes

1. Luke 14:25–33.

2. "Elders, Boomers, and Their Parents," *CNN Money*, July 29, 2005, http://money.cnn.com/2005/07/28/retirement/legacy_survey/index.htm.

3. Stephen R. Covey, *The Seven Habits of Highly Effective People* (New York: Simon & Schuster, 1989).

CHAPTER FIVE

VALUABLES AS VEHICLES FOR VALUES

Teaching Your Legacy

"Imagine a man," the Teacher smiled around at his listeners, "who kept a rich man's books." The faces looking back at him showed little evidence of firsthand experience with accountants or rich men or balance sheets or wealth sufficient to need "keeping."

"He was not an honest man, I fear," the Teacher regretted. "I'm not sure how he managed to get his job in the first place. He fudged the accounts. He found small ways, subtle ways to steal from his master. He made poor investments. He frittered away the rich man's wealth."

The faces around him smiled at that. Everyone enjoys a good crime story!

"But, apparently, he was not as subtle or as smart as he thought. His master learned about his mismanagement, confronted him, and gave him the boot."

"What did he do?" someone from the crowd wanted to know.

"Well, now, that's the interesting thing." The Teacher wagged his finger as he made his point. "He didn't plead innocence. He didn't apologize or beg for second chances. He realized he had just one shot to provide for himself and his future."

"He stole what he could on the way out the door!" another voice suggested.

"In a way," the Teacher nodded. "But in a very smart way. He brought in everyone who owed his master and encouraged *them* to steal: 'Tear up that bill for eight hundred gallons of olive oil and replace it with a bill for four hundred' . . . 'Throw away this invoice for a thousand bushels of wheat and write a new one showing you owe much less.'"

"How would that help him?" an old man wanted to know. "It's the debtors who profit, not the manager."

"True enough," the Teacher smiled. "But debtors have a way of being grateful to those who reduce their debt!" He waggled his eyebrows at the crowd, a hint of mischief in his expression. "This man knew he faced a hard future. His job was gone. He didn't have the stomach for manual labor. And he was too proud to beg. So he put his master's debtors in debt to himself!"

The quicker listeners in his audience began to nod and smile. "Oh," they said, the light dawning.

"Yes," Jesus nodded back. "He used money that was not his to make friends. By letting these debtors off the hook, he created an obligation. When he needed food or a bed or a handout, all he had to do was go knocking at their door. 'Remember me?' he'd ask them. 'I took care of you, once upon a time. Now it's time for you to take care of me.'"

"He wasn't a very nice man, was he?" someone muttered.

"No, he was not," Jesus acknowledged. "But for all his failings, he was shrewd about the ways of the world. If the rascal had simply stuffed his pockets, his master would have thrown him in jail. But what could the master do now? Accuse his friends and business associates of thievery? Question their accounts and their honesty? What proof would he offer? The old receipts were gone. The new books balanced perfectly.

"In the end, the master could only admit he'd been bested. He even *commended* this scoundrel on his plan. 'You are one unpleasant fellow,' he told him. 'But at least you know how to use money to make friends. You know how to spend in the present—even if it was my money you spent!—to take care of your future. Well done! Now get out!'"

Jesus stopped talking. He let the story hang above the crowd while they tried to see the sense in it.

"I don't understand." Even the sharpest among his listeners seemed confused. "Are you telling us it's OK to steal, to act dishonestly?"

"Certainly not!" Jesus insisted. "I'm telling you that even honest people—especially honest people—need to be shrewd about the way they handle this." He held up a coin and showed it to the crowd. "If you handle this shrewdly, if you use it for higher purposes, God will trust you with more important matters. Be wise with money," he waggled the coin, "and money will teach you to be wise about things that are truly valuable."

"Do you understand?" he asked them.

They didn't. Most of what the Teacher said went over their heads. But no one said that out loud.[1]

Affluenza

There is no necessary correlation between the ability of someone to make a fortune and the ability of his or her children and heirs to enjoy a healthy relationship with it.

In fact, the one recurring problem among people who have inherited wealth is that most of them end up struggling to come to grips with the effects of this "sudden money." That's because who we were the day before the inheritance was received is who we are the day after. We have the same strengths, the same flaws, the same habits. Character is not *improved* by a sudden receipt of money. It is *revealed* by it. If we didn't have a healthy relationship with money before we became rich, if our values don't go deeper than our valuables, that relationship will only grow more problematic as we find ourselves suddenly awash in money.

There is a reason nine out of ten inheritances fail: the best inheritance plan cannot compensate for an unprepared heir. When money is the primary focus of estate planning, inheritors often confuse their self-worth with their net worth.

In *The Golden Ghetto: The Psychology of Affluence*, Jessie O'Neill (herself an heiress of a wealthy family) describes the impact a financial inheritance can have on people who receive valuables without the sustaining values of a legacy—that is, money without meaning.[2] She lists the following outcomes of a condition known as "affluenza," defined as a dysfunctional relationship with possessions.

- Inability to delay gratification
- Inability to tolerate frustration
- Low future motivation
- Low self-esteem
- Low self-worth
- Lack of self-confidence
- Lack of personal identity
- Social and emotional isolation
- Feelings of depression, failure, anxiety
- Unrealistic expectations
- Lack of accountability
- False sense of entitlement
- Inability to form intimate relationships

Jamie Johnson, heir to the Johnson & Johnson fortune, diagnosed a similar malaise while filming the 2003 documentary film *Born Rich*. He interviewed ten fellow heirs, including Donald Trump's daughter Ivanka and Michael Bloomberg's daughter Georgina. The movie portrays the very real and very common dangers of "money without meaning," including drug abuse, inability to work, and the paralyzing fear of disinheritance. Johnson came to the sad realization that so many of the heirs he knew were unsuccessful despite having every advantage.

People who receive valuables without accompanying values are especially susceptible to such dangers. They catch affluenza pretty easily. Take an emotional five-year-old. Give her lots of gadgets, luxuries, and material resources. Do you really expect that to be a recipe for maturity and emotional health?

The very idea of affluenza flies in the face of what most people believe their lives would be like if, one day, they came upon the proverbial pot of gold. "If only I had money," the fantasy begins. "People would like me. I would be respected. I would be free to do whatever I wished, whenever and wherever

I wanted to do it. I could take charge of my life, and I would have a sense of absolute security. Nothing could intimidate me, and I would have power. Real power. Most importantly, I would be happy."

It's a great fantasy. An enormously seductive illusion.

Close your eyes and imagine discovering that you have inherited one hundred million dollars from a long-lost uncle. You can immediately satisfy your every desire. You have the wherewithal to buy any home, consumer toy, piece of art, luxury automobile, or companion. Jet to Fiji tomorrow? Why not? Spring in the south of France? Dinner at Maxim's? Whatever you want!

If the opportunity to indulge every fantasy, every whim, every physical or emotional desire should drop in your lap, what would you do? Say, "No, I'm not ready"? Ask for a little time to better prepare yourself to handle wealth maturely? Recognize that your personal pleasures are not the first priority in a world full of needs and hurts?

Or would you succumb to affluenza?

William K. Vanderbilt (1849–1920), grandson of the "Commodore," spent his life engaging in leisure sports such as yachting, auto racing, and horses. His summer home at Newport, Rhode Island, was modeled after the *Petit Trianon* at Versailles. It featured five hundred thousand cubic feet of white marble and custom furnishings from Paris. He employed a staff of thirty-six maroon-liveried butlers, maids, coachmen, and footmen.

Vanderbilt's lavish lifestyle was extraordinary, at least for its excess. How he felt about the impact of his family's wealth on his own life was another matter. He wrote to a favorite cousin: "My life was never destined to be happy. Inherited wealth is a big handicap to happiness. It is as certain death to ambition as cocaine is to morality."[3]

Andrew Carnegie, the nineteenth century steel magnate and billionaire (back when a billion dollars meant something!) understood the effect of unearned money on heirs. In a letter to a friend, Carnegie wrote: "The parent who leaves his son enormous wealth generally deadens the talents and energies of the son and tempts him to lead a less useful and less worthy life than he otherwise would.[4]

Bucking the Trend

Most parents pass along to their children almost everything they've accumulated over a lifetime—in spite of the risk of spoiling them rotten or ruining their prospects for a productive future. But, increasingly, there are people who are bucking that trend.

When Warren Buffett pledged thirty-one billion dollars to the Bill and Melinda Gates Foundation in 2006, he rekindled a debate among the rich over inheritance: whether it's better to limit what you pass on and protect your heirs from the ravages of affluenza, or let them inherit the wealth and try to build on it. Buffett has famously said that wealthy parents should leave their children with enough money to do anything they want but not so much that they are doomed to do nothing at all.

Bill Gates shares those sentiments. He founded Microsoft in 1975. For the next thirty-three years, he worked hard to build the company . . . and to amass one of the largest fortunes in history. (Actually, he is currently slotted at Number Two on Forbes's list of the world's wealthiest individuals—after Mexican Carlos Slim—only because he's already given away twenty-eight billion dollars of his fortune to charity.) Like Warren Buffett (his friend and mentor), Gates has publicly stated that the majority of his wealth will be donated to the Bill and Melinda Gates Foundation.

But what about his kids? Gates is determined they will receive only a "miniscule" portion of his total wealth. "They are normal kids now. They do chores, they get pocket money. . . . They will be given an unbelievable education and that will all be paid for. And certainly anything related to health issues we will take care of. But in terms of their income, they will have to pick a job they like and go to work."

You probably aren't stratospherically wealthy like Buffett or Gates. But even those of us who are only marginally or moderately "wealthy" should think about the risks involved with passing on possessions to our heirs. Are those risks unavoidable? Are we condemning our children to debilitating bouts of affluenza when we provide a financial inheritance to them? Or might there be a way to *prepare* our heirs to receive our valuables by grounding them in the values that give those valuables meaning?

Hard questions:

- How much inherited wealth would it take to *harm* a child—to encourage habits and attitudes that cause damage rather than blessing?
- Will inherited wealth be more likely to strengthen the faith of your heirs or undermine and weaken their faith?
- What have you done to prepare your heirs to receive an inheritance that will bless (rather than cripple) them for a lifetime?

Gates and Buffett model one approach to protecting your family from the dangers of affluenza—give most of your wealth away so your children won't run the risk of being ruined by a too-large inheritance. Another approach (advocated here) suggests that the real danger to your family is not inherited valuables but un-inherited values. What inoculates our heirs from the ravages of affluenza has less to do with the amount of their inheritance than with a definition of "inheritance" that goes beyond the merely material. We have better things to offer our children than a bank account. We have heritage, faith, life-wisdom, principles, goals, and character. If we work as hard to pass on matters that matter as we work to pass on money, we can protect our families even as we provide for them.

But how? In thinking about such important questions, I believe Jesus gives us some guidance.

A Material Means to a Godly End

The parable that begins this chapter suggests we should understand (and teach our children) that money is a means to an end. Money must be used with *tomorrow* in mind, not to hush the endless yammerings of *today*.

But the parable does something more. It points to *how we teach that lesson*. There is a hint—hidden at the end of the story—that suggests a way to move our kids from focusing on money per se to learning the kind of shrewdness that will help them handle money (and life?) well.

Is shrewdness teachable? (It's certainly *not* a virtue commonly extolled by Christians!) Can we prepare our heirs to use money purposefully and for a cause greater than themselves? Jesus thinks so.

> Whoever can be trusted with very little can also be trusted
> with much, and whoever is dishonest with very little will also
> be dishonest with much. So if you have not been trustworthy in
> handling worldly wealth, who will trust you with true riches? And
> if you have not been trustworthy with someone else's property,
> who will give you property of your own? (Luke 16:10–12)

Jesus (as always) teaches some good stuff here. But the one truth we should focus on (for our purposes at the moment) is the *ordering* Jesus suggests. Notice where he begins . . . and where he ends. He starts with the material and the tangible, and then moves to the personal, relational, and spiritual. He suggests that if we build character in our children through their interactions with money, we'll have a chance to build our children's character in more important matters (such as marriage, relationships with other people, perspectives on faith, principles to live by).

Jesus is saying (bluntly and boldly) that valuables provide a vehicle for teaching values. Talk about money—help those you love use money wisely, with tomorrow in mind—and you'll have a chance to talk about the values that build a good life. Here is the principle: show someone how to be trustworthy in handling possessions, and they will demonstrate trustworthiness where it really counts.

Many parents tend to reverse that order: first show kids how to handle faith, ideals, and relationships (the "true riches" of life) and *then* they'll learn to handle money. "If we can just build integrity into our kids, a strong work ethic and compassion for others, then they will be equipped to handle the inheritance when the time comes." In a word, we start with values and arrive (eventually) at valuables.

So we take our kids to church. We quote pithy maxims at them. We read Bible stories and "values" books to them. We preach the importance of virtues and integrity and good deeds. We warn against bad habits and bad companions. We start with principles and end with possessions. We teach character lessons and hope our kids will apply those lessons to their use of money.

All of which we (Dan and Tim) strongly support. All of which we did ourselves. We see the sense of putting things in this order: values *then* valuables.

The two of us were never above doing a little "preaching" when it came to shaping the character of our kids.

But you have to admit it is interesting that Jesus starts with the material and suggests that valuables are a good way to get at values. It's as if he is telling us: "Equip your kids to handle money, to use it wisely, to be shrewd about material things, and they will learn lessons about integrity, a good work ethic, and compassion. Those lessons will help them with the rest of their lives."

"Trustworthiness"—Jesus seems to say—"is a trait that cuts its teeth on dollars and cents, not on high-minded ideals or highfalutin concepts. If people won't learn the practical lesson of handling money wisely, they'll never learn the more subtle skills required for the really important things of life."

An Example

One of the families we work with puts this principle into practice. The parents (for years) have set aside a certain amount of money annually (say, one thousand dollars), dedicated to their children's use. The kids can do what they want with the money: throw a party, buy toys, travel, save, invest, give the money away to charity. The kids decide what to do with it.

There are a few conditions attached, however—some rules the kids must observe:

1. The kids must make the decision about how to use these funds *together*.
2. The decision must be unanimous and enthusiastic.
3. Their discussions in making that decision must be reported in writing.
   - What options were considered?
   - How was the final decision made?
   - Where did the money go?
   - What were the measurable results?
4. The funds must be "tracked." Receipts. Returns. A paper trail.
5. An end-of-year report must be submitted to the parents.

It's the next "wrinkle" that makes this family exercise so interesting. Every year, the parents review their children's use of these funds. They determine how "successful" the kids have been—how shrewd—by employing certain criteria (which the kids understand). Was the decision about the money, in fact, unanimous? Were all the kids "on board" with the decision? Any dissenters? (The more unity and enthusiasm, the more "credit" is given to the kids.)

Enthusiasm	5	4	3	2	1	Caution

What were the key factors driving the decision about how to use this money? Were any of those factors related to family values (such as time together, investing wisely, compassion for those in need, or encouraging worthy works)? (The more connected the use of the money is to family values, the more credit goes to the kids.)

Family Value	5	4	3	2	1	Other

What was the goal of the decision? (Spend the money? Give it away? Invest and grow it? The more difficult the goal—spending is easy!—the more credit.)

Difficult Goal	5	4	3	2	1	Easy Goal

Who benefitted directly from this decision? The kids themselves? The family as a whole? Others not connected to the family? (The less "selfish" the benefits, the more credit they get.)

Selfless	5	4	3	2	1	Selfish

If the money was invested, did the investment prove profitable? And, if so, what was done with the principal and profit at the end of the year? (More credit for good investment decisions, less for losses.)

Profit	5	4	3	2	1	Loss

Did the decision about the money reflect values and priorities of the parents (not just the kids)?

Parent Values	5	4	3	2	1	Other

Did the decision result in "making friends" for the family in the future?

Friends	5	4	3	2	1	No Friends

In the parents' opinion, did the kids prove "trustworthy" in their use of these funds?

Trustworthy	5	4	3	2	1	Untrustworthy

On the basis of these criteria, the parents decide the kind of vacation the family will take in the coming year.

The first year they began this exercise, the kids took the thousand dollars and bought themselves iPhones and a Nintendo. The family vacation was a week of car camping at a local state park—hot dogs and instant oatmeal. Time together, certainly, but not everyone's favorite vacation memory!

The next year, the kids invested the money in a hot stock and made a two-hundred-dollar profit. At the end of the year, they rolled half of the total (six hundred dollars) into a CD to seed future plans and donated the other half to a favorite family charity. That year, the family went skiing in Colorado.

"We wanted to give our kids the chance to manage a little money," the parents told me. "We wanted them to do this cooperatively, as a team. We hoped they would think about this opportunity with some higher goals in mind, more than their immediate wants and desires. We wanted them to make decisions from a family perspective.

"When we're gone," Mom and Dad look at each other and smile, "they'll inherit a lot more than a thousand dollars. We just pray they'll remember some of the lessons they learned with a little so they can be faithful in handling much more."

From Cents to Sense

Jesus talked about money and material possessions all the time. There are at least forty separate teachings involving money recorded in the Gospels (see Appendix A). Do you know why he talked about money so much? Because people *listen* when this subject comes up. Material possessions are a subject they understand and appreciate. There's something so concrete about possessions, so graspable, so relevant.

And Jesus consistently used this subject to get at more important things. He brought up money so he could talk about how God provides (Matt. 6:11, 31–33), the importance of trusting God (Matt. 6:19–21), the place of money in God's value system (Matt. 23:16–17; Luke 9:25), the dangers of greed (Mark 4:19; Luke 6:24–25; Luke 12:15), the role of generosity in a disciple's life (Luke 6:30–38), and the futility of worry (Luke 12:22–23)—among other things!

Money was a common theme in Jesus' teaching because it allowed him to get at matters that, to him, really mattered.

You have a legacy you want to pass on to your kids. The largest and most important part of that legacy involves the values that formed and guided your life . . . the values you hope will form and guide the lives of your heirs. However, if you wait (as most people do), until your will is read to see whether your heirs handle their inheritance in a "trustworthy" manner—well, you won't be around to see it, will you? It will be too late then.

We are suggesting that the valuables accumulated over your lifetime may be a God-given opportunity to help your heirs become trustworthy—in things small and large. By using the subject of possessions, inheritance, and money, you have a chance to shape your heirs *in the here and now* to be trustworthy in the future.

We're not talking about manipulation or control or string-pulling. We're not suggesting holding money over your heirs' heads to get them dancing to your tune.

We're talking about recognizing that money is a tangible subject that people are eager to talk about . . . and that discussions of money often lead to unexpected places, charactered places, that allow you to talk about the values that matter most.

Vague principles, discussed in theory, without application or practical use, have little appeal to most people. (A reality upon which many a sermon has foundered!) But when we talk about money with our children, when we place valuables in their hands to handle, when we trust them with the material to teach them about the spiritual, suddenly they're all ears. They listen eagerly. They open themselves to our input. They may even open themselves to our wisdom.

The process outlined in the chapters to follow describes a way to partner practically with your heirs in preparing them for their inheritance. It begins with the material and moves to more important matters. It starts with your valuables and gives you the opportunity to teach values.

That process invites your heirs to hear stories about how you made your money, the sacrifices that were made, the challenges and failures you experienced. You'll tell tales about their ancestors and the family traits you inherited that led you to be financially successful. You'll show them how you use your money and the commitments you try to honor as you invest, spend, and donate it.

You will help your heirs experience using money in godly ways: sharing material blessings through hospitality, generosity, acts of compassion, tithing, and philanthropy. They will do more than listen; they will participate in these ventures themselves, partnering with you, learning from you.

And the process will encourage deep, collaborative, meaningful communication within your family. That communication will begin by focusing on material things: your will, their inheritance, life insurance, business assets, and so on. But conversations about the material set the stage for more substantive discussions: family values and traditions; their hopes for the future; what they want to pass on to their own children; causes the family believes in deeply enough to cooperate on and make financial commitments to; the role of faith in their lives and the convictions they have embraced.

In these conversations, your heirs will have a chance to listen to you. But you will also have a chance to listen to them, to assess where they are and what they need. Perhaps most importantly, your heirs will have a chance to listen to each other and begin the difficult work of hammering out a working relationship that can outlive you.

In these and other ways, the process we describe in this book will help you help your heirs. Like the manager in the parable, they will have an opportunity to use money that is not yet theirs with tomorrow in mind. They will be offered the chance to use money for purposes greater than today's comforts and desires. They will demonstrate whether they can be trusted with material possessions . . . whether they can use money *shrewdly*. As they make this attempt, you get to assess whether they have learned the lessons needed to manage your greatest bequest: the broad and deep legacy you want to leave them.

Exercises

1. In this chapter, we listed a number of symptoms of the material disease affluenza. Are any of these symptoms showing in your own family?
2. Are there any tangible, material decisions to be made in your family in which you intentionally include your family in the decision-making process? What are those decisions? How is your family included?
3. List ways in which this mutual decision making has brought your family together.

Notes

1. Luke 16:1–12.

2. Jessie O'Neill, *The Golden Ghetto: The Psychology of Affluence* (Milwaukee, WI: The Affluenza Project, 1997).

3. Jerry E. Patterson and Harry Abrams, *The Vanderbilts* (New York: 1989).

4. Andrew Carnegie, *The Autobiography of Andrew Carnegie* (Boston: Northeastern University Press, 1986).

A LEGACY PROCESS

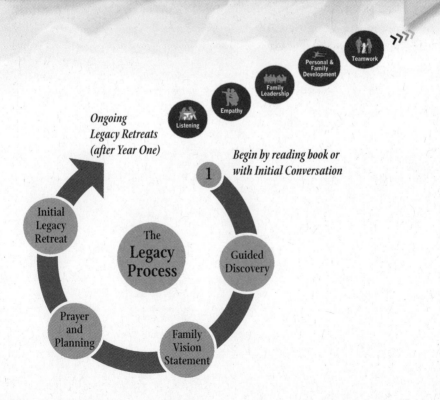

Ongoing
Legacy Retreats
(after Year One)

Begin by reading book or
with Initial Conversation

Listening

Empathy

Family
Leadership

Personal &
Family
Development

Teamwork

1

Initial
Legacy
Retreat

The
**Legacy
Process**

Guided
Discovery

Prayer
and
Planning

Family
Vision
Statement

Only you can decide whether to be intentional about the legacy you leave with those you love. Apart from a basic will (distributing assets), most people choose (by default) to let their lives speak for themselves. "Here is the smorgasbord of my life," they effectively say. "Pick through your memories, impressions, inklings, and hunches, and take what you want as a legacy from me."

If you decide to be more intentional than that, we can help. You don't have to start from scratch or reinvent the wheel. There is a process we have used with hundreds of families to plan for and build a future. It isn't easy (being intentional is *never* easy). It isn't quick (you don't pass on a legacy overnight). It isn't simple (the devil, as they say, is in the details). If you want easy, quick, and simple, may we suggest Burger King?

But if *legacy* is your goal, and your *loved ones* are your focus, there is a proven process available for you as you attempt to pass along both your valuables and your values. We call it the *Legacy Process*. Think of it as a path cleared through the jungle of the future. Hundreds have walked before you, proving the trail, moving with purpose and direction, leading their families toward tomorrow.

You can buy a machete and clear your own trail if you want. But the blood, sweat, and tears we've invested in the Legacy Process suggest that you might want to walk with us, learn the lessons we have discovered, and avoid the bogs we have slogged through. Only you can decide to be intentional. But you don't have to go there alone. You are not limited to your own resources once you choose the intentional path. We can help. And that help begins by talking you through some of the details of the Legacy Process.

CHAPTER SIX

INTRODUCING THE LEGACY PROCESS

"You've no idea how much I have looked forward to eating this Passover meal with you before I enter my time of suffering."
(Luke 22:15 THE MESSAGE)

Jesus could have let his life and teachings speak for themselves. He could have allowed the apostles to sort through the last three years and decide what was most important, most basic, to Jesus' legacy. He might have concluded that, if they hadn't grasped the fundamentals by now, another evening and one more conversation wouldn't do much good.

Instead, Jesus plans for a Passover meal with his closest companions, one more chance to drive home the themes that have driven him: I am the way . . . remain in me . . . love each other . . . live by the Spirit . . . be my witnesses . . . expect persecution . . . stay faithful to the end.

A final meal. A concluding conversation. An opportunity Jesus had planned and anticipated for a long time. The Last Supper was not just a photo-op or a friendly farewell or a closing ceremony. It was an occasion for Jesus to emphasize—one more time—the essentials he wanted his followers to take away from his life.

As we eavesdrop on the Last Supper, we are watching Jesus write the legacy he intends to leave behind with those he loved best.[1]

Who Will Write Your Legacy?

Whether by design or by default, you *will* leave a legacy. Some trace of you will remain after you pass. It may be as faint and short-lived as the last snowflake of spring or as strong and enduring as a granite mountain. The nature and impact of that personal legacy on future generations, and whether you will leave a legacy that is *intentional,* is one of your most important life accomplishments.

Unfortunately—due to procrastination, lack of time or motivation, and countless other distractions—legacy is a decision often left up to family members or friends, usually determined about the time they are picking out your headstone. *Others* will sort through the details of your life—your strengths and weaknesses, your successes and disappointments, your ideals and goals—to determine the extent and the character of your legacy. *They* will pick the principal values you leave behind. *They* will determine the lessons to be taken from your life. And they will do it on the basis of limited memories, personal biases, incomplete information, and the assumptions and prejudices everyone brings to the table.

The question is not whether you will leave a legacy but *who will write it.* Do you want to leave your legacy to chance . . . or do you want the chance to shape the legacy you leave? Do you want something more than an accidental legacy . . . a legacy unplanned and unintended?

Epitaphs are the inscriptions on tombstones commemorating the lives of the people buried beneath. And they provide a snapshot into the importance of *intentionality* as people consider what they want to say to the future. Go wander through a graveyard for a few moments and look at the weathered basalt columns and ornate stones that mark the graves of people just a little farther down life's road than you.

Some tombstones indicate a complete lack of planning for sending a message to the future. Look how many inscriptions include nothing more than a name, a date of birth, and a date of death. Unimaginative. Bland. Sterile. A whole life summed up with a moniker and a time frame.

Some tombstones were obviously written *about* the person lying beneath, summaries of a life offered by others. There is a tombstone in Maryland that has neither name nor dates. Just this somber statement: "Here lies an atheist. All dressed up and no place to go." I read once about a tombstone for a Wells Fargo agent in (ironically!) Tombstone, Arizona: "Here lies Lester Moore. Four slugs from a 44, no Les, no more." Humorous, perhaps, but a sad summary for a life.

On a few tombstones, however, you will find an epitaph written by the person buried beneath . . . an intentional message left behind for the challenge and edification of those who visit their tombs. Winston Churchill's inscription on his gravestone at St. Martin's Church: "I am ready to meet my Maker. Whether my Maker is prepared for the great ordeal of meeting me is another matter." From Robert Frost, the poet? "I had a lover's quarrel with the world." I like Sir Walter Raleigh's epitaph, written on the night he was beheaded: "Reader—Should you reflect on his errors, remember his many virtues, and that he was mortal."

What is true of tombstones is true of legacy—*someone* is going to write a summation of your life. It may be a stranger chiseling out some bare-bones factoids about you . . . or a family member raking through your life to choose which lessons to learn from you . . . or you—deliberately and intentionally— saying something about yourself to be remembered long after you are gone.

No one is better equipped to write the legacy of your life, to list the lessons you have learned, to highlight the values you honored more than *you*. *You* are the one who lived your life. And *you* are the one to examine your life closely enough to recognize the foundations on which it was built.

"Isn't that self-serving?" you might ask. "Isn't this just an exercise in trying to manage the way I am remembered by my heirs?" It could be. No doubt many people who mold their own legacies are moved by less-than-stellar motives: hiding faults and failures . . . whitewashing flaws . . . airbrushing unpleasant realities. You may be one of these people. Your efforts may be motivated less by legacy than by lies. That's something best left between you and God.

But for people of good motive—for those of us who really want to distill the essence of our own lives because we long to pass on something helpful, something useful, to those we love—the issue is really whether we are willing to *own* our personal legacy. Will you and I take responsibility for the lessons and learnings of our lives, and do the hard work of sifting through the details and detritus of life to find the pearls that have formed around our scars and successes?

Here are your options:

1. Ignore your legacy and refuse to think about the messages your life will communicate.
2. Leave the legacy of your life for someone else to write (friend or foe, wise man or fool).
3. Construct a lie for a legacy—pass on some pretty words that have little relationship to the life you've actually lived . . . worry more about image than impact.
4. Take responsibility for your legacy and pass on something genuine, effective, and transformative.

Legacies are never written by perfect people—people with no mistakes in their pasts, no detours along the journey, no scars on their faces. But it's better that imperfect people (like you and me) shape the legacies we leave behind than abandon that task to the unpredictable efforts of people who knew us partially and imperfectly.

A New Process for Legacy?

The data, the research, and our own experience clearly show that most inheritance plans fail. Gaining a consensus on that fact among people in the estate planning industry has never been a challenge—there are no takers for the argument that traditional estate planning builds strong families across generations. Traditional plans aren't designed for that purpose. Something better, deeper, and more extensive is required.

We determined to address this need. Recognizing the need, however, wasn't enough—in itself—to build a new kind of planning model. Listing the limits of traditional planning models was only a start in the right direction. Much more was required.

1. We had to redefine the traditional view of "wealth" to include more than money and assets.
2. We had to consider the values, virtues, and traits that not only contributed to a client's material success but also helped make his or her life meaningful and fulfilling.
3. We had to take into account the reality of family dynamics, such as strained relationships, sibling rivalry, immature heirs, poor communication skills, the difficulties of discussing money, feelings, and faith.
4. We had to construct a practical, achievable framework that would promote family strength, unity, and involvement, while encouraging individual excellence and achievement on the part of family members.
5. And we had to make the resulting process one that could be taught to, and replicated by, other professionals.

No small feat.

With these things in mind, a process for thinking and talking about legacy began to emerge. Slowly. Painfully. It was based on established practices but still a matter of trial and error over the years.

Certainly, we wanted to help people pass on their valuables, to take care of—financially, materially—the people they loved and the causes and organizations in which they believed.

But our aim was higher. We also wanted to help people pass on their less tangible (and vastly more important) values:

- The lessons they have learned in life.
- The people and ideas that helped them succeed.
- The opportunities they have seized (and the ones they squandered).
- The skills that proved most valuable in building a life, family, or business.
- The role patience and persistence have played in their endeavors.
- The sustaining power of faith.
- Their hopes for their family's future.

Traditional estate planning does not, and cannot, address these matters. That's not what it is designed to accomplish. A different process, asking different questions, utilizing different methods, and pursuing different goals was needed.

As we began the long journey of research and development, some of our colleagues argued that a broader process would never work. "Too ambitious," some said. "You can't use an inheritance to do parenting," others objected. "A few conversations won't change a family," the pessimists declared.

And as we started to focus on family health (not just family wealth)— to see the significance of family stories and traditions, the importance of faith and feelings, the power of ideals and values and principles—even more doubting Thomases came forward. "Too fuzzy," they said. "Too touchy-feely. You'll never be able to talk about that stuff with families. Stick to the spreadsheets and leave the psychoanalysis alone."

Many advisors had reservations, cautions, and qualms; although none of them (not one attorney, CPA, planner, or nonprofit executive!) ever said a different process wasn't needed. Nobody took the position that "the estate planning system ain't broke, so why fix it?"

On the contrary. The best, most successful and accomplished advisors in the nation (representing many of the most affluent families in America) agreed that the traditional system does a wonderful job of passing assets and minimizing taxes, and a terrible job of preparing heirs to receive their material inheritances.

Our task, therefore, was to develop and refine a process that could meet the "show me" test of the toughest advisors before it could ever be put to work for the clients they represented. It had to be based on solid scholarship, implemented by highly qualified and experienced advisors, and, most of all, it had to make sense to the families who needed it.

The Legacy Process

Here is what we came up with. Here, in a nutshell, is the Legacy Process.

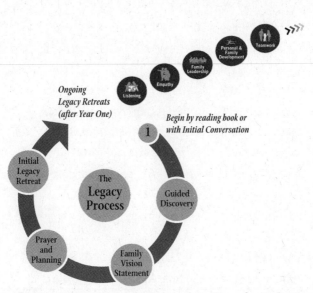

The process begins with a very personal exploration of your heritage (where you came from), your influences (what shaped you), your life story (what happened to you), and your life lessons (what you learned). We refer to this as the **Guided Discovery**—a process for asking questions that are foundational to your legacy.

From this personal exploration comes an initial document: a **Family Vision Statement**. It is a document that records what you discovered about your ancestors and influences and values. It is a document that, in many ways, tells the story of you. But it is more. It is also the story of your family— its past and (hopefully) its future. Family traits and family commitments. Family mission and goals. This document will change with the input of your children and loved ones (as it should). But it is your "stake in the ground" . . . the starting line for passing on a legacy to your family.

Once your Family Vision Statement is done, you'll need to spend some time **planning**: to share your story and vision and values with your family . . . to encourage your heirs to embrace those values, adopt that vision, and carry on the story in positive ways. In this part of the process, you think through the challenge of transforming intentions into realities.

Now you are ready for an initial **Family Retreat**. We call this a "pre-inheritance" experience. It's a chance for your family to sit down and talk about matters that matter. Money and what your heirs can expect (in general terms) to inherit from you. But so much more: your family's history and heritage; the key traits that have defined and (hopefully) will continue to define members of your family; some significant lessons you have learned and hope to pass on; your affection for and trust in the family you will (one day) leave behind.

At the conclusion of this *initial* retreat, you will make plans for ongoing **Family Retreats**, annual meetings of your family and heirs to ensure that the foundation you laid for the future gets the walls and windows and roof that make the future livable. Think questions, reactions, discussion, affirmation, education, sharing, buy-in, planning, commitments.

In the chapters that follow, you will see how our conclusions about the failure of traditional planning and inheritance and about money and values have been forged into a dynamic process that is grounded on both solid academic research and real-world experience.

You will see how:

- Focusing on things of value, rather than on the value of things, translates into multigenerational legacy plans designed to combat the Ninety Percent Rule.
- The best toolbox you have for building a sustainable future for your family is one you already carry around everywhere—your own life and learning.
- Confession, testimony, honesty, encouragement, and sharing are as necessary to shaping family health as wills, spreadsheets, and asset-assessment are to passing on family wealth.
- A detailed plan—written down, processed, prayed over—can become a roadmap for reaching the destination of family health, wealth, and vitality.
- A Legacy Process Partner (helping you develop and work that detailed plan) can be as important to the long-term future of your family as traditional planning advisors, attorneys, charitable giving officers, and CPAs. (You'll find a list of recommended facilitators at the end of this book.)

- "Communication, communication, communication" is the family-planning equivalent of "location, location, location" in real estate.
- An active program of family philanthropy may be the most constructive means of building bridges between family members, and ensuring family unity, that has ever been envisioned.

You can write the story of your life. You can shape the legacy you leave to those you love. You don't have to face the future of your family with fingers crossed and bated breath. You can give them the best of yourself—intentionally, thoughtfully, prayerfully.

If Jesus thought it important to pour the essence of his life and teachings into an explicit and carefully planned conversation about values and character and faith—to impress his core legacy into the hearts of his apostles as his life drew to a close—how important should a similar exercise be for you and the future of your family?

Someone will determine the character of the legacy you leave behind. Why can't that someone be you?

Exercises

1. Picture yourself seventy-five to one hundred years from today . . . you are no longer here. If it were possible to look back, what would you like to see your heirs doing . . . being . . . accomplishing?
2. What is the most valuable thing you can give (or hope to give) your heirs? If you could pass along only one gift to the future, what would it be?
3. List at least five *values* (not *valuables*) you hope and pray will live on in future generations of your family.
4. What are you doing *today* to prepare your heirs to carry on your gifts and values after you're gone?

Note

1. Luke 22:7–38; John 13–16.

CHAPTER SEVEN

YOUR GUIDED DISCOVERY

"Whoever has ears to hear, let them hear." (Mark 4:9)

Sometimes he wondered whether anyone was listening.

It didn't matter how large the crowds were. It didn't matter how they craned and gawked. All they cared about was what he could *do*. "Heal us." "Feed us." "Show us a sign."

Oh, they listened well enough when he told them stories. But they didn't understand what they heard. Even his disciples were bewildered by his stories. He had to take them aside and explain everything . . . slowly . . . with small words.

Most people were patient enough when he taught. They even called him "Teacher." But words were such ephemeral things. They left his mouth and hung briefly above the crowds—like morning mist. Then they melted away, and he wondered whether any words actually lodged in hearts and lives.

He knew his words took hard work to hear. They made listeners *think*, search themselves, and ask the kinds of questions most people avoided. They forced people to consider higher horizons, troubling topics, eternal issues. It was the rare listener who was willing to work that hard.

Jesus sighed. Then, lifting his voice above the cries for help and bread and attention, he opened his mouth and began to teach once more.[1]

Your Guided Discovery

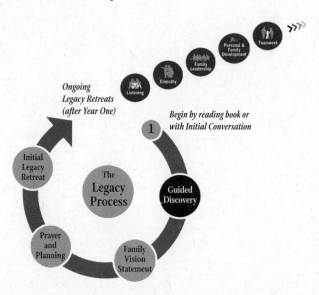

The first step in the Legacy Process will take you on a journey unlike anything you have experienced. Through Guided Discovery, you will work through a structure and process that allow you to identify, reflect on, and communicate the values and traditions that have shaped your life. Throughout this Guided Discovery, you will focus on the memories of ancestors, the life lessons you have learned, the character traits that have proven valuable, and the mentors who shaped you—the nuts and bolts that have contributed to the legacy you want to pass along.

Guided Discovery will require you to ask the kinds of questions most people avoid, to contemplate higher horizons. It will oblige you to trust in the power of words—not just what you can *do* for your heirs but what you hope to *tell* them. It will mean you must believe your heirs are listening and will take your words to heart.

The process of Guided Discovery (and sharing what you discover with your loved ones) won't be easy. It won't be painless. Not everyone is willing to work this hard. But it will be worth it. Because the result will be something that captures the best you have to offer those you love most. Not just a few dates and accomplishments. Not just the "who, what, where, and when" of your life. But the all-important "why."

For many, the Guided Discovery will be the first time to reflect (in a formal way) on childhood, education, work, significant mentors, children, the future, and the other important issues that constitute a true legacy.

At the heart of the Guided Discovery is the idea that you must be an active, exploring, curious, and contributing participant. This is not a lecture in which you passively receive a flow of information. You will make discoveries about yourself *for* yourself. You will surface your highest hopes and dreams for the future of your family. You will begin to identify the greatest gifts you have to offer the ones you love. No one is better equipped to shape this legacy than *you*.

Still, you'll probably need help. You don't have to go through this process alone. There are facilitators who are available and equipped to walk you through a Guided Discovery. The single best gift you could give yourself and your family as you think about your legacy would be securing the services of a trained, experienced, and skilled personal guide. If you have the financial resources, a facilitator will get you started well, help you move forward efficiently and effectively, and encourage you to reach your legacy goals.

Included at the end of this book is a list of recommended facilitators. If you want to make a meaningful investment in your family's health, we encourage you to look over this list, check references, choose a facilitator, and invite him or her to partner with you in your legacy adventure.

If, on the other hand, you prefer a DIY approach to the Guided Discovery, we have included a number of resources. Consider this chapter a "virtual guide" to the discovery process; it provides an overview of the areas you need to explore, suggests questions to ask and information to gather, and invites you to write down and formalize what you learn. We have included (in Appendix D, *Chapter Seven Exercises*) questions, checklists, and tables to help you work through the Guided Discovery on your own. There is even a workbook available online for your convenience at www.garrettgroupinc. com/legacyworkbook or www.theacufoundation.org/legacyworkbook.

Back to the Future

What does the process of Guided Discovery actually entail? We start with the *Legacy Matrix* (below)—a graphic encouraging you to identify and reflect on the key influences that have shaped and guided you: heritage, family, faith, and so on.

The Legacy Matrix

Guided Discovery is an exercise in *memory*. It is designed to help you sift through a lifetime of experiences and relationships and commitments. By recalling stories, making lists, naming names, identifying core attributes, and asking good questions, you will create an awareness of your personal and family wealth. (Remember that the definition of wealth is not just about money!) The awareness developed through this process provides an understanding of your hopes, dreams, desires, goals, values, and moral beliefs sufficient to create your Family Vision Statement (the focus of the next chapter).

As you walk through the Guided Discovery, you will probably find yourself coming to new levels of understanding and appreciation (those great, brain-stimulating aha moments!) about:

- Yourself and your family.
- How you became the person you are today.
- What role your parents, grandparents, and other important people in your life played as you matured.

- How the best (and, sometimes, the less-than-best) those people contributed to your life has been filtered through you to your own children and grandchildren.
- What success and accomplishment and money mean to you.
- And, most importantly, what kind of clear, unambiguous legacy you desire to leave to generations of your family to come.

Guided Discovery is about going "back to the future." Before you can move forward *intentionally*, you have to go "back" . . . into the past . . . into your heritage and history. By acts of memory and acceptance and appreciation, you build a foundation for your family's future.

The past is your first step to legacy.

The Hebrews understood this. Every Passover, they prepared a future by going back to their roots. They recalled the times of slavery and suffering. They remembered God's compassion and intervention. They recited the story of the blood on the doorposts, the Death Angel, and striking out into the wilderness. They did this deliberately, purposefully, with the future in mind:

> When you enter the land that the LORD will give you as he
> promised, observe this ceremony. And when your children ask
> you, "What does this ceremony mean to you?" then tell them, "It is
> the Passover sacrifice to the LORD, who passed over the houses of
> the Israelites in Egypt and spared our homes when he struck down
> the Egyptians." (Exod. 12:25–27)

The early Christians understood this. Every week, they prepared for the future by going back to their roots. They celebrated "the Supper," a remembrance of Christ's death and burial and resurrection. They recalled the cross and the tomb. They did this deliberately, purposefully, with the future in mind: "Whenever you eat this bread and drink this cup, you proclaim the Lord's death until he comes" (1 Cor. 11:26).

In similar fashion, we can move purposefully into the future by recalling our roots and acknowledging the debt we owe to our ancestors and family of origin . . . to the people who took us under their wings . . . to the faith that nurtured and guided us . . . to stories of our own successes and disappointments.

Heritage

You probably have one or more around the house. In the hall closet, under your bed, or stuffed into an attic trunk. Old binders, with cloth-covered cardboard jackets, exuding the faint, musty aroma of age. You're careful when you lay them out on the kitchen table, cautious about turning the brittle pages. Someday, you'll make copies. Someday, you'll scan the photos into your computer and add captions so that your grandchildren can name the faces that peer silently from across the decades. Someday.

We know the names of some of the people in the photos, but other faces are strangers to us, mysterious phantoms from a vague past. There is a grainy photo of the great-grandparents, fresh off the boat. Why is grandmother standing in front of that church? Who is that woman holding Uncle Carl's hand? Where was that farm in the photo? ("I didn't know our family owned a farm!") Oh, there's Grandpa's brother, the one who started the family business.

Look again at the black-and-white photo of great-grandfather. He worked night and day to provide basic food and shelter to his family, sacrificing his own dreams so that one day his children would have a better life. Photos of Grampa and MaMa, struggling to hang onto their farm during the Depression, sustained only by sweat and faith and sheer, dogged determination. Then Mom and Dad with those silly grins, standing so proudly in front of their first house.

If we don't see—and appreciate—that the old family photos are a living history of the value and meaning of character, faith, endurance, and hope, we are missing one of our family's greatest legacies. The values by which your forebears lived are, without question, among the most significant and useful assets you possess. More valuable than real estate, investment portfolios, and cash savings. Because right there, in the unvarnished, honest faces of the generations who came before you, is the key to understanding most of what you need to keep your family strong for generations to come.

We begin by creating a personalized map of your ancestors . . . a genealogical chart of your extended family. In Appendix D is a chart (*Our Family Tree*, 211) that lets you name your parents, uncles and aunts, grandparents, and great-grandparents. Most people have a hard time filling out this chart from memory. There are likely to be gaps and questions. A little research might be required to capture this visual representation of your family history. But the journey to legacy starts by telling your family's story. And you can't tell that story if you don't know the cast of characters. So go on. Start filling in your family tree right now.

Once you have the bare bones of your heritage, it's time to supply some details: traditions, achievements, facts and legends, characters and characteristics. We have included a few questions and prompts (*Our Heritage*, 212–213) to help you dig deeper into your family of origin and the significant impact passed on to you through your heritage. Go to Appendix D now and spend some time digging through the gold mine of your past.

Family

Your *extended* family shaped and influenced you in ways you may never have realized before. But your *immediate* family is an even more important part of your story. In fact—for most of us—our immediate family is the *point* of our story . . . the reason we have decided to think so carefully about legacy.

Can you remember the face of your spouse on your wedding day? How excited you were to buy your first home together, take your first vacation, welcome your first child into the world? Can you see your daughter's eyes, reciting her lines in the school play . . . your son running the bases? What hopes you had for them! How proud you felt, how full of undiluted love!

Now ask yourself: What did it mean to be "family" in your family? What were the special traditions you kept, the habits you cultivated together? Did you go camping? Spend afternoons on the trout stream? Cook Thanksgiving meals together? Watch football? Perhaps the movies, with coffee afterward to dissect what you'd just seen?

Special memories will lead you to significant insights. "I've always thought that if I could teach my children to work hard, everything else would follow." "I want my son to know I love him, will always love him no matter what." "I'm so proud of my wife. She is the best person I know." "Trust and obey—like the old hymn says—that's what I want most for my kids."

Tread carefully, respectfully, when you step into such territory. This is "holy ground" stuff. You are closer here (in contemplating your immediate family) to identifying the nature of your legacy, the true riches of your life, the "what" you want to pass on and the "why," than in any other memories or influences you might explore.

We have included some questions and prompts (*Our Immediate Family*, 214–215) in Appendix D to help you think about your family story. But don't limit yourself to this list. Spend as much time as you can reflecting on your family relationships and values. Gather some old photos, drawings and awards, notes written to you by your kids. Recall a few funny stories, a handful of poignant recollections, about each member of your family. A little effort at this point pays real dividends later on!

Faith

If you are reading this book, your faith plays a significant role in your life: influencing what you believe, your worldview, your understanding of life's meaning and purpose, and the moral compass by which you navigate. You have a relationship with Jesus. You study the Bible. You go to church.

Do you have a story about a time when prayer saved your sanity? Have you ever felt the Holy Spirit move? When did God keep his promises to you? Do you have a favorite Bible

verse? What is it about this verse that speaks to you? Do you have a favorite hymn? What is it about that hymn that speaks to you?

Your faith is an important part of your legacy—no matter how well or poorly you may have expressed that faith in your day-to-day living. You don't have to be a spiritual giant to pass on a spiritual legacy. Scripture testifies that even flawed people can hand off a spiritual compass to their children. Sometimes, the best saints are the ones with dirt on their hands and stains on their robes.

As you examine the influence of faith on your life and family, you'll see how intimately connected faith is to legacy, how faith *roots* legacy in the eternal, how faith transforms your values from "personal preferences" and "common sense" into timeless principles.

The worksheet *My Faith* (215–216) includes some questions and exercises to help you *think* about the role of faith in your legacy. But, the ultimate purpose of these questions is to help you *talk* about faith with your family . . . to give your heirs a chance to hear plainly and unambiguously what faith has meant to you and what you hope it will mean to them. For too many families, faith is implicit—something assumed but rarely talked about. In families serious about legacy, however, faith is explicit—something openly talked about and actively pursued. Use these exercises to reflect on your personal and family faith. As you do so, however, imagine yourself discussing these things with your children.

Life Lessons

Perhaps you remember a book entitled *All I Really Need to Know I Learned in Kindergarten,* by Robert Fulghum. Published in 1988, short and sweet, it sold millions of copies. Even five-year-olds, Fulghum suggests, have enough life experience to understand important principles like:

- Share.
- Play fair.
- Don't hit people.
- Clean up after yourself.
- Say you're sorry when you're wrong.

The title of Fulghum's book, however, is misleading. You *do* learn important lessons about life early on. But you don't learn *everything you need to know*. In fact, the essence of wisdom involves being a "lifelong learner"—as committed to learning about life at ninety as at five.

Here are a few life lessons that might appear on the list of a ninety-year-old—lessons no self-respecting kindergartner would (or could!) include:

- Life isn't fair, but it's still good.
- It's okay to get angry with God . . . he can handle it.
- Make peace with your past so it won't screw up your future.
- No one is in charge of your happiness but you.
- Growing old beats the alternative.

You probably aren't ninety years old. But you certainly are not five! You have plenty of life under your belt. You have seen and done a great deal. You've experienced highs and lows, victories and disappointments, hard times and easy street. You've known comfort and loss, pain and pleasure, grief and joy. You have the scars and smile lines of living on your soul.

With all that life behind you, what have you learned? Could you make a list of the most important lessons life has taught you? What has the University of Hard Knocks shown you that you would never have learned in kindergarten? With all that accumulated wisdom, are there any simple, straightforward observations you would pass on to your family?

The exercises in the *My Life Lessons* worksheet (217) help you identify the hard-won wisdom that has meant the most to you . . . that guided and guarded you along the way. By "naming" them and then writing them down, you take an important step to passing them on.

Successes and Setbacks

Everyone can point to some success of which they are particularly proud or grateful. And everyone has some measure of disappointment that saddens but sharpens them. These successes and setbacks say much about what you

attempted in life, the boldness with which you lived, and the ambitions that drove you. But, far more important than the successes or setbacks themselves, is the way you *handled* these experiences. What you *did* with achievement or loss, with goals gained and missed, says much about who you are and shaped the kind of person you eventually became.

Your children, like you, will experience highs and lows. The people they become will be decided not by the proportion of successes to setbacks, but by the manner in which they respond to each. What would you want your heirs to know about the importance of celebrating victories and shrugging off defeats? How can success be dangerous? How can disappointments point toward a brighter future?

The exercise *My Successes and Setbacks* (218) will give you some guidance as you reflect on these important questions.

Mentors

"No man is an island, entire of itself." We all float in a sea of other people, significant people, people who have influenced and guided, taught, and led us. You haven't thought about some of those people for years. You may not have realized (except on reflection) the debt you owe to certain people for their care and input.

Certain people have made a significant difference in your life. The lessons you learned from them have left an indelible mark. In a similar manner, your children and grandchildren will be marked by the people they meet. Acknowledging your influences, recognizing the people to whom you owe a "character debt," will help your children look for and appreciate the people in their own lives who have much to teach them.

Think through different areas of your life, the people who most influenced you in those areas, and the most significant lessons you learned from them. The *My Mentors* chart (219–220) will help you identify the people who have shaped you and the kind of influence they had on you.

Character Traits

You have character traits that are . . . well . . . *characteristic* of you. Traits that reside at the core of your personality. Qualities that define you. Not all of them are necessarily positive—even the best of us has our flaws. But there are certain parts of you that *you* could not do without and still remain *you*. In fact, when you think about it, these characteristic qualities have much to do with what you have achieved in life, your successes and accomplishments, your victories against the odds, your contributions and reputation.

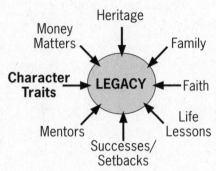

In the complexity of temperament, gifts, traits, and attributes, there is a core of characteristics—a handful of traits—that is central to your personality. Affability. Optimism. Loyalty. Persistence. Can you name the two or three qualities that comprise the heart of you? The two or three qualities that have contributed most to the life you have lived?

Your heirs will share some of these qualities. Embedded in their character will be some of the same traits that mattered so much to you. Those traits may need to be honed and sharpened, developed and matured. But you can encourage that process by shining a light on particular attributes and giving testimony to their impact on you.

So give some thought to your own character, to the personal qualities that have shaped your life, and to the traits you would commend to your children. A checklist and a few questions in the *My Character* exercise (220–221) at the end of this book will help you do this.

Money Matters

Last (and, honestly, least) comes a little reflection on your financial legacy . . . the possessions and material things you want to pass to your heirs. Money is where most people (and most estate planning models) begin. List assets. Reveal portfolios. Disclose net worth. Create trusts. Devise inheritance instruments.

It is easy, with such a beginning, to think of "legacy" primarily in terms of finances. But, if you've been with us this far, you know that legacy is far broader (and far more valuable) than anything that can be reduced to dollars and stock options.

It is a grave mistake to begin your legacy discussion with money. But it is also a grave mistake to be so high-minded about your legacy that you never get around to discussing money with your heirs. In fact, your financial bequest is an important component of your legacy.

The very existence of significant assets validates the values and traits that generated it. The love and respect indicated by your desire to pass those assets on to your heirs creates an openness on the part of your heirs to thinking about a wider legacy. The realization that your heirs are not simply inheriting money from you but the family's name and reputation, the desire to make a difference, the faith and traits that are vital to the family—the weight of such a legacy helps your heirs take their inheritance seriously.

In order to complete the Guided Discovery, you need to be able to think and talk about money: how you made it, how you saved it, what it has permitted you to do, your sense of stewardship, the attitudes toward money you'd like your family to demonstrate, what plans have been set in motion for passing your assets on when the time comes. *Our Money* (222–223) is an exercise that has been included to help you work through legacy issues related to your material assets.

Conclusion

The success of your family depends not just on planning for the future but on recognizing and applying the lessons of the past. A legacy is defined by a history—a very personal and particular history—not by the value of your assets or the size of your bequest.

Estate planning and accounting procedures do not offer a fraction of the wisdom, courage, strength of character, or good sense of the family, friends, and mentors who have touched your life. The finest investment advice and best-selling business books cannot touch the profound life lessons you've gained through hard-won experience and deeply embedded traits. TV talking heads on money management and the market can never grant your loved ones what your own journey and faith and insight have uniquely equipped you to give them.

In the next chapter, you will use these discoveries to write a meaningful obituary—a summary of your life—to pass on to your loved ones. It won't be a brief paragraph listing facts and places and dates. It will be an obituary worth reading . . . something that serves as your "manifesto" . . . a written guide for your children . . . your "voice" after you are gone.

If you've taken this Guided Discovery process seriously, you'll have spent significant time examining yourself, scouring your memories, and answering important questions. No doubt it's been hard work, time consuming, even personally painful. Not everyone is willing to listen to life, examine oneself, and contemplate the future to this depth. But your investment is about to pay off. The more care you've exercised in the Guided Discovery, the more equipped you'll be to map out a path for your family's future. You will have all the building blocks needed to begin translating your hopes, wishes, dreams, desires, and goals into a solid foundation that can sustain your family across generations.

Like Jesus, you may still wonder whether anyone is really listening. You may be overwhelmed by the clamor of your family's demands for you to *do* something . . . underwhelmed by their willingness to hear what you *say.* In the end, only those who have ears to hear will have the heart to listen.

Whether your loved ones ever hear you is—ultimately—up to them. Giving them something *worth* hearing is up to you. The process of Guided Discovery is where the worthiest part of yourself is put into words for those who have ears to hear.

Exercises

The *Chapter Seven Exercises* are included in Appendix D. They include worksheets to help you think through your heritage, immediate family, faith, life lessons, mentors, character, and so on. Samples:

- What were the characteristics you most admired in your parents?
- What would you identify as your single greatest success or accomplishment?
- What character trait is most "characteristic" of you?
- Do you practice the habit of generosity? To what extent?

Note

1. John 6:25–66; Mark 4:34.

CHAPTER EIGHT

YOUR VISION STATEMENT

"Would you tell me, please, which way I ought to go from here?"
"That depends a good deal on where you want to get to," said the Cat.
"I don't much care where—" said Alice.
"Then it doesn't matter which way you go," said the Cat.
"–so long as I get SOMEWHERE," Alice added as an explanation.
"Oh, you're sure to do that," said the Cat, "if you only walk long enough."
—LEWIS CARROLL, *Alice's Adventures in Wonderland*

He knew they didn't understand where he was going.

He'd told them . . . plainly. "Jerusalem." But the disciples didn't want to hear. It was dangerous there. The religious authorities were waiting for him . . . looking for him. They'd made threats. They'd laid plans and schemes. It was no secret how the Jerusalem elite felt about Jesus, what they wanted to do to him.

Even when he left Galilee, leading them south along dusty roads, the disciples were relieved when nothing actually changed: the Pharisees kept pestering; the crowds still thronged; Jesus taught and healed as always. They turned east and crossed the Jordan, away from Jerusalem. More parables. A gaggle of children. A rich, young man who went away sad. It was business as usual for Jesus, his disciples thought.

Only it wasn't. He kept returning to Jerusalem in his thoughts and words, brooding on the events about to unfold, determined to reach that difficult destination. "Jerusalem," he kept telling them. "Betrayal and arrest and death." Still they didn't want to hear. They changed the subject. They hoped for the best. One of his closest companions told Jesus, in a firm tone, to think happier thoughts.

But one day, he turned west again. Across the Jordan to Jericho. A day's tramp from there to Jerusalem itself. Jesus walked with a determined stride. They could not distract him. They could not dissuade him. "Jerusalem!" he told them and marched ahead.

They did not understand the destination because they would not understand the goal. Jesus was a man with mission on his mind. He knew what he had to do. And, thus, he knew where he had to go.

The disciples did not understand. But they would.[1]

A Map of the Future

Do you know where you want to go? Do you have a vision of where you would like to lead those who follow in your footsteps? Of what is worthy of commending to future generations? Do you have a destination toward which you can aim your life and your family?

Imagine a map spread on a table before you. On the map are places to journey . . . different routes by which to travel . . . a list of hazards and prospects along the way . . . a catalogue of benefits and drawbacks when you arrive.

Only *this* map is not defined by geography or compass points or physical roads. It is defined by hopes and dreams, by aspirations, by values, and by principles. The paths it charts are not paved with asphalt but with character and traits, attitudes and commitments. And the destinations it describes have nothing to do with towns or terrain, but with meaning and significance and joy and love.

Like Moses, we are all seeking a Promised Land. You may not know the details of that land, the dimensions and design. But you know it is out there, in front of you. You've been traveling toward it all your life.

Also like Moses, you may never reach that Promised Land yourself. Your life may end short of the destination. That's not the point. You have others who are traveling with you, family who mean more to you than your own life. The Promised Land is for *them*. Your job is not to *arrive*, but to *point the way* to those who walk with you, to excite them about the destination, to encourage them to continue the journey.

If you took the last chapter seriously—if you did the hard work of Guided Discovery—you've already marked your "life map" in monumental ways.

- You've traced the route your ancestors traveled before you—the detours and challenges, the mountains climbed, the comforts left behind in search of a better place, the stories of your heritage.
- You have identified the general direction in which you have traveled personally—by pondering your faith, the principles by which you lived, and the mentors who shaped you.
- You've placed a large X on that map to indicate the present location of your family: what it means to be family, your traditions and rituals, the values that form the core of your home, the habits you share.
- And, most importantly, you've pointed to the desired destination—the hopes and dreams you have for your family's future, the values and valuables you entrust to them to help them along the way.

Well, at least, you've made important and useful marks on your *personal* map. But the marks are in pencil. There are cross-outs and erasures and blots and marginal notes. In places, your handwriting is illegible. There are gaps on the route that need bridging.

A personal map is good. But if you want a map to guide your *family*—a clear diagram that will help them navigate an uncertain future—you need to "formalize" the route; chart the path in bold, red ink; write your cautions and encouragement in a firm hand; and signify the destination in unmistakable ways.

You need a Family Vision Statement that shows the way forward to those you love best.

A Vision for Your Family's Future

Be daring, be different, be impractical, be anything that will assert
integrity of purpose and imaginative vision against the play-it-safers,
the creatures of the commonplace, the slaves of the ordinary.
—CECIL BEATON

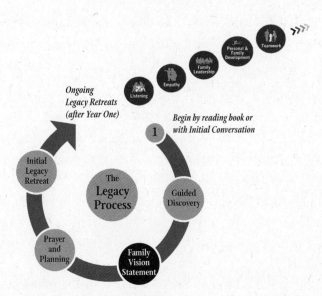

Take a brief survey of the most frequent inscriptions carved into the marble
and granite facades of public buildings, churches, monuments, and memori-
als all over the world. If your results are similar to ours, the most commonly
inscribed quotation comes from the Bible: "Where there is no vision, the
people perish" (Prov. 29:18).

The quote is carved on the Peace Tower in Ottawa, Canada. Members of
the British House of Commons pass beneath this quote as they enter their
chambers. It was Abraham Lincoln's favorite maxim.

Vision matters, and people who want to shape the future understand
that. The ability to perceive the world around us and to develop a vision
which defines and directs our lives is one of our greatest capacities. Humans
possess no greater power than being able to conceive and bring to fruition
the visions that shape their destiny. This uniquely human ability enables
the artist to create, the scientist to discover, the tinkerer to invent, and the

businessperson to build. Vision is the fuel for the engine that has fired all human achievement since the dawn of time.

Vision is equally critical for families. Families perish for lack of vision. Not for lack of trying or lack of resources or lack of good intentions. Lack of *vision*. Families without vision bumble into the future without guidance or direction. They "make it up" as they go along. They take any road. They follow the path of least resistance.

Vision steers. It inspires. It leads. In the best of times, vision lets us stride forward with confidence because we know where we are going. In the tough times, when our way gets confused and the path peters out, vision helps us stay the course and persist through difficulties.

Without vision—clear, compelling, common vision—your family won't walk in the right direction . . . they'll stop when they should keep going . . . they won't stay together for the duration of the journey.

The most significant gift you can give your family is a legacy that results from vision.

I just used three words—clear, compelling, common—that are important at this stage of the Legacy Process. In order to impart a vision to your family that is effective and influential, your vision must be all three of those things.

Clear. It is not enough to pass on a *modeled legacy and vision*. While you cannot lead your family to places you are not willing to go yourself, neither will you lead your family without *expressing*—in words!—the destination you hope to reach. Clarity requires you to move beyond wishes and hopes and vague yearnings . . . to find tangible words, state unambiguous goals, and express explicit directions and expectations. Much of this chapter involves helping you translate voiceless groanings into concrete nouns and verbs.

Compelling. Even if your vision is clear, if it doesn't motivate and inspire, it will not lead. Some destinations are just not worth the effort. If your vision aims too low, if it does not challenge and excite, it cannot urge your heirs to make a significant difference. One of the most important lessons you have learned by thinking about legacy is that "making more money" or "protecting the wealth you have inherited" is not a compelling vision. Something more, something greater, is needed if you want to give your family a vision that not only explains but excites. In this chapter, we'll help you paint pictures rather than cite facts, tell stories rather than list objectives. We'll help you aim higher—for the sake of your family.

Common. In the end, "your" vision must become "our" vision. What begins as a private vision must morph into a vision held in common. A vision that is not embraced and adopted by your family is no more than a *personal* dream—good only for as long as you draw breath. It cannot become the guiding compass for subsequent generations. A vision statement can be clear and compelling. But if it is not *owned* by your children and grandchildren, it is just words and aspirations, not the practical guide you need to help your family navigate the future. The next two chapters will help you create a sense of ownership in a Family Vision Statement by those who will rely on that vision after you are gone.

As you worked through the Guided Discovery, you identified and reflected on the values you learned from your heritage and other important influences in your life. You thought about faith and character traits and the lessons you gleaned from life. You put money in its proper place and affirmed the truly valuable things about living: family, relationships, purpose, meaning, impact.

The point of all that work was to prepare you to create what can become the most important family document in the lives of your inheritors: your Family Vision Statement. More significant than a will, more defining than a stock portfolio, better reading than trust documents (hopefully!), this testament to your family's heritage and hopes can make a radical difference for your family's future.

Its purpose is to shine a bright beam of light down a straight path, to provide a map that leads the way, to inspire and instruct generations to come. It is more than a family history and different from a legal contract. Your Family Vision Statement positions your family to act as a team in future decision making. At the same time, it describes how family members can support and contribute to one another as individuals within that process. In helping generations of your family understand their heritage from the past, your Family Vision Statement provides a foundation for family unity in the future. By using the family's own values and traditions as building blocks, your Family

Vision Statement becomes a credible, unique, and powerful resource that can be embraced by succeeding generations.

There is no correct form the statement must take, no rules of style or structure to which it must adhere. The length, breadth, and depth of your statement will be a function of your own story and the guideposts you wish to communicate.

That said, there are some blueprints (and resources) available to help you write this statement.

As with the Guided Discovery itself, there are facilitators who are skilled and experienced at helping you write a Family Vision Statement that is clear, compelling, and consensual. They have done all this before. They know what works and what doesn't. They understand some simple rules for writing, such as, "Keep it short," "Keep it simple," and "Show, don't tell."

If you have the financial resources, a facilitator can help you craft a statement your family is more likely (and more eager!) to read and embrace. (Included at the end of this book is a list of recommended facilitators.)

Should you prefer a more hands-on approach, the rest of this chapter is intended to be a "virtual guide" for making a good start on your own. There are ten steps you can take on the path to writing your Family Vision Statement. We've included some helps and hints for taking these steps in Appendix E: *Chapter Eight Exercises*. Along the way, we've provided some personal examples (in italics)—just so you can catch the flavor of a meaningful Family Vision Statement.

Step One: The Purpose of Your Family Vision Statement

Start with a letter (or video) to your family and heirs. Explain what the Family Vision Statement is about, what it involves (an overview or summary), why it is important, and the role you would like to see this document play in the life of your family's future.

- Keep it short (one typed page? a couple of minutes?).
- You sent a similar message—to your great-great-grandchild—in Chapter Four. With a few modifications, that first attempt could serve as the basis for this one.

- You might want to borrow some of the material that introduces this chapter (e.g., the Lewis Carroll quote) to incorporate into your letter.
- Write a sentence or two (a "testimonial") about the importance of these matters in your own life.
- Recognize this is not a finished document: the members of your family will have a chance (at the Family Retreat) to discuss, edit, and adapt the contents to themselves and for their future.

A sample opening paragraph: *Dear Family, we are placing this document in your hands because we love you more than anything else in the world. We want you to inherit the most important treasure we have to give you: some hard-won wisdom. This wisdom comes from the generations that precede you, from a foundation of faith and values, and from the lessons we've learned on the road we have traveled together. It is the most valuable thing we can offer you. We hope, as you read and reflect, that you will recognize its value and embrace the accumulated wisdom of our family. "Pay close attention to what your father tells you; never forget what you learned at your mother's knee. Wear their counsel like flowers in your hair, like rings on your fingers" (Prov. 1:8–9 The Message).*

Step Two: Heritage

Do you realize you may never have told your family's story *to your family*? Oh, you've related random memories, talked about certain ancestors, given glimpses and clues into the past. But nothing comprehensive . . . orderly . . . thorough.

I recently sat down with my parents and asked them to talk about their family history. It was . . . interesting. First, I recorded the session on my iPhone. The resulting video was a hit with my siblings and has become a family treasure. Second, I learned things about my family's past I'd never known before—places, personalities, struggles, accomplishments. Third, I was surprised at how limited was my parents' awareness of their own family history: Mom and Dad could not name their great-grandparents, for example . . . they had only the vaguest knowledge of our ethnic and national roots.

Take the Family Tree you completed during the last chapter's exercises and the insights into your heritage you jotted down (the *Our Heritage* exercise), and write out a biography of your extended family—a chronicle of your family's history. Remember: you are creating a narrative, not listing facts. You're telling a story your children (and theirs!) will want to read, not inflicting another chore on them.

The Garrett name comes from a combination of Old German words (gar meaning "lance" or "spear" + hard meaning "brave" or "strong"). Our forefathers were (most likely) soldiers who crossed the English Channel during the eleventh century in one of the Norman invasions of the British Isles. The Garrett family emigrated from England in the 1600s. Five generations lived in southern Alabama.

We've included an outline (*A Heritage Biography*, 225–231) in Appendix E that you might want to follow as you write your heritage history.

Step Three: Your Personal Story

Learning about your family's history is fun. But telling your own story is where this process gets personal. Your family needs to know your story if you expect them to embrace your legacy. But (as with the story of your family's heritage) they may never have heard you talk about *yourself* in an organized, intentional way. They've gotten bits and pieces, dribs and drabs. But not the story from beginning to end . . . not the story from your own lips.

Where did you grow up? What do you remember about your childhood, your first job, your first romance, your first hobby? How did you do in school? When did you and your spouse meet? What was your courtship like? How did you begin your career? What was the high point of your working life? The low point? What does "success" mean to you, and (as significantly) what does it *not* mean?

In this section of your Family Vision Statement, you have the great opportunity (and rare privilege) of telling your story to generations of your family. Obviously, you have more story than paper. Perhaps a few tips would be in order.

- Keep it *short*. Better a few pages that will be read than a tome gathering dust!

- Keep it *significant*. This is not the place for random memories or "slice of life" ramblings. As you sort through the details of your life, you must select the details that matter, that have shaped you, and that will mean something to your heirs.
- Keep it *positive*. You are not writing a confessional. Don't burden your readers with your dirty laundry. (We all have it, but this is not the venue for airing yours.)
- Keep it *dynamic*. While a few dates and places are appropriate to your life's story, the truly compelling part of your story are the *stories*. Unpack your memories. Paint portraits of the people who shaped you. *Show* your family what it was like to grow up dirt poor, or in a foreign country, or with more aptitude for math than sports—don't just *tell* them about it.

1968 was a turning point in my life. I had been living in Washington State, working for Green Giant, and farming wheat. I was just treading water and needed to make some significant changes in my life. So I returned home to Florida and attempted to reenter college. 1968 was the height (or depth) of our involvement in the Viet Nam war. I needed to be in school. But, with very poor grades from a former fling with junior college, no university would accept me. A family friend wrote a beautiful letter of recommendation, however, and I was able to enroll at David Lipscomb College (now Lipscomb University) on probation. It was there I met Donna Nadeau on a blind date and, later, persuaded her to become my wife (forty-three years and counting!). Through my wife and others at Lipscomb, I came to know the Lord Jesus in a very profound and personal way. In 1968, my life changed for the better and has never been the same since.

We've included a few suggestions—an outline—for writing your life story (*My Autobiography*, 227–228) in Appendix E.

Step Four: The Story of Your Immediate Family

Your children have been part of your family ever since you became a family. But there are large and significant parts of the family story they were present for but do not remember (their early years). There are important and defining parts of the family story they may know but need to be reminded of (the themes that are woven through the fabric of your family's narrative). They have been a part of your family's story, but they do not *know* that story like you do.

So *tell* them. Sing the song of your family. The birth of your children. Where the family lived. What gifts and talents you saw developing in each of your kids as they grew up. What traditions and rituals you kept. What activities you engaged in together. Family values and traits.

We loved to backpack when you kids were younger. Campfires and s'mores and fishing in remote streams. But you wouldn't know we loved it listening to the moaning and whining on the trek in. We developed a mantra for the trail that you kids would say with me as we hiked: "No complaining. One foot after another. Keep your eyes on the horizon." Actually, now that I think about it, that's a pretty good philosophy for life!

Once again, we've included an outline (and a few examples—*Our Family Story*, 229–230) for you to consider as you write a brief history of your family in Appendix E. Remember to keep your reflections *short, significant, positive,* and *dynamic.*

Whew! You are almost there! Most of the hard work is behind you. The next steps are much shorter and will take less time.

Step Five: Faith and Values

Faith plays a significant role in your life. You believe certain things that shape what you value, the way you conduct yourself, and the manner in which you treat other people. You've made commitments to God that require discipline and sacrifice.

Have you talked to your family about your faith? Openly? Fully? About the importance of faith to you, personally? About why your family prays together and goes to church on Sunday and practices compassion and generosity?

You've already done some good thinking on the role of faith in your own life and in your family (see your notes on the *My Faith* exercise from the last chapter). If you had one page to write about the importance of faith, one page to explain your personal testimony and faith walk, what would you include?

Before we started our family, we prayed that—if we were blessed with children—they would grow up to be faithful servants in the kingdom . . . that they would marry Christian mates who would help and encourage them on their eternal journey . . . that if our children eventually had children, they would raise and train our grandchildren to love and serve Jesus. We are grateful for God's faithfulness in answering those early prayers.

Now look through your notes on the *My Life Lessons* and *My Successes and Setbacks* exercises from the last chapter. Are there any nuggets of wisdom about life you would like to pass on to your children? Any boiled down, top three, essential pointers you would give them? It won't do any good to list the twenty-five most important things you would like them to know about successful living. They'll be overwhelmed. They won't read or remember so long a list.

But if you could choose just a handful of fundamental principles, ideas, maxims, or rules for living, what would they be? Write them down. Pass them on.

"You reap what you sow," says the Bible. I believe that. Perhaps not right away. And probably not every time (thank goodness!). But eventually the habits and attitudes we develop bear fruit and produce consequences in our lives. A wise friend once told me, "Good habits are hard to form but easy to live with. Bad habits are easy to form but hard to live with." Be sure to plant good habits. You'll like the harvest.

Step Six: Character and Significance

In Chapter Seven, you were asked to list the people who have influenced your life and what kind of influence they had (an exercise called *My Mentors*). As you look over that list, who would you consider your "top three" mentors, and what did they teach you? Write their names down. Summarize (in a sentence or two) the lessons you learned from them. Say a word to your heirs about what these people and these lessons have meant for your life. Would you encourage your kids to seek out mentors of their own? Tell them.

You also reflected on the personal characteristics that have served you best and that you recognize in (and would commend to) your loved ones (the *My Character* exercise). Identify one or two characteristics or traits that have contributed the most to your life, traits you hope to pass on to those you love.

Growing up as a teenager, money was always tight. Early on, I mowed lawns and had paper routes to earn money for clothes and (eventually) dates. I purchased my own bicycles and lawn mowers. Arvie Allison gave me my first real job. I worked after school and on Saturdays. He helped me realize and believe I could make something of my life. His confidence and encouragement helped me dream of a better and brighter future for myself.

Step Seven: Our Definition of Wealth and the Desired Effects of Our Children's Inheritance

How do you measure "wealth" in your family?

- *Financially*? (A list of possessions or the amount in your bank account?)
- *Intellectually*? ("Members of our family are smart and curious. The old saw is particularly true for us: We think, therefore we are.")
- *Emotionally*? ("As a family, we tend to mature early, build intimate relationships, and see past ourselves to others. This is our defining and most valuable family trait.")
- *Spiritually*? ("We are a family that puts God first and values heavenly treasure above all else. Circumstances change. Money comes and goes. But the 'Word of the Lord stands forever.'")

Does your family equate wealth with the ability to afford any luxury or with the responsibilities for others and for the wider community that come with financial blessings?

In a world that is consumed with material wealth—gaining it, holding it, spending it, trusting it—it is important for you to help your family recognize the place of valuables in the wider context of values.

Once again, you've already done some deep thinking about the role of money in your own life and in your family's priorities. (See your notes on the *Our Money* exercise.) Summarize your thinking on values and valuables. Encapsulate it. And then give it to your children in easy-to-swallow, cherry-flavored form.

I've worn much-patched jeans (as a necessity, not as a fashion statement!) and very expensive suits; driven clunkers and Audis; lived in shacks and mansions.

Frankly, having money makes life so much easier. But it doesn't necessarily make life better. *Only you can build a good life, a productive life, a happy life. Money won't build that kind of life for you.*

Many parents express their hope in this section that the material inheritance they leave their children will not turn them away from the core values that will ultimately determine the fate of individuals or even the entire family.

Jesus once said, "What good is it for someone to gain the whole world, yet forfeit their soul?" We can't leave you the "whole world." But we will leave you what we can. We're glad for you to have it. We want you to enjoy it. Just don't imagine that money can be an adequate substitute for true *treasure: faith, family, character, wisdom. If gaining your inheritance means losing yourself and each other, we will have failed you.*

Step Eight: Our Financial Objectives

Many people are surprised to learn that the Family Vision Statement doesn't spend much time or take up much space addressing concerns about taxes and financial bequests, bank accounts and business succession plans. While details about possessions and financial inheritances are important (certainly to the heirs!), parents who want to create a vision for their family's future tend to focus on matters more necessary to the family and its long-term well-being. Consider just a few of the financial objectives parents define for the well-being of their families.

We hope your inheritance gives you the opportunity to:

- Establish a lifestyle and standard of living that is secure, healthy, and free from fear.
- Attain a quality education that will make you productive and independent.
- Take time to explore, travel, and discover your best gifts.
- Work hard because you love what you do rather than merely because you need a paycheck.
- Take risks, follow your dreams, build something.
- Establish a secure home and provide important necessities for your family.

- Spend quality, memory-making time with brothers and sisters, nieces and nephews, cousins—all the people who share our family bond.
- Be generous to those in need, to worthy causes, to your church and other ministries, and to efforts that ease some of the suffering of this world.

Personal comfort and financial security are important, and most people make that clear in this section of their Family Vision Statement. But inheritance objectives limited only to the coziness or convenience of heirs are too narrow in scope. You have a chance to set a larger horizon for your family as they think about managing the inheritance you leave them.

What are your objectives for handing off material assets to your heirs? Take a few moments and write down half a dozen. (You can borrow from the list above, if you want!)

Money can't buy love. But it can give you a little time. I inherited a small sum from your great-grandfather. Enough to give me three months to knock around Europe, see the sights, and experience life in different cultures. Best education I ever got! Best investment I ever made! Use your inheritance (at least part of it!) to take the time to travel, try on a couple of jobs before you settle on one, discover what you're truly good at.

As my father taught me, "It's not what you make or inherit that matters—it's what you do with what you make or inherit." Money is simply a medium of exchange. You can't eat it. You can't even burn it fast enough to keep you warm. So "exchange" it for things that will make you wiser, better, broader, and more interesting.

Step Nine: Balancing Our Children's Outright Inheritance with Their Charitable Inheritance

Many parents express hopes that an inheritance for their heirs will afford those heirs the opportunity to pursue personal goals. But, as a result of the Guided Discovery process, parents are also convicted of the importance of wider goals and higher aspirations than the merely personal.

Generosity and liberality, charity and philanthropy, play important roles in the lives of many who have been blessed with financial means. A virtue that is first expressed almost by accident—good-hearted people with unanticipated means sharing with others in need—grows quickly into a habit as those people experience the joys of generosity.

Through Guided Discovery, people become aware (often for the first time) that they've gotten *liberal* over the years. They give freely. They enjoy donating of their means. They look for opportunities to encourage and sustain ministries and missions. They adopt worthy causes and support them with money, time, and energy. Generosity has come to mean a great deal to these people. It has become an important component of the way they manage material wealth.

The French speak of *noblesse oblige*—the idea that privilege entails responsibility. Most of us would state the same idea in less lofty terms: "We are blessed to bless." Of course, there are those (like modern-day Scrooges) who hoard their money, squirreling it away for selfish purposes. They won't be parted from their hard-won earnings, no matter how good the cause!

But more people recognize their financial plenty is as much the result of "blessing" as of "earning." They were at the right place at the right time. Someone was watching over them. They were "gifted" with certain attributes and talents. (We will explore this idea further in Chapter Twelve.)

To honor this blessing, they feel the need to bless in return. So they tithe to church. They help a neighbor in need. And they find a cause to give themselves to.

As you consider your legacy, consider how *philanthropy* (the "love of man") fits into it. Is it enough for you to pass along your blessings to your heirs? Or will you pass along the responsibility to bless in turn? Will you encourage your heirs to experience the joy of generosity?

You may even come to recognize the power of philanthropy not only as a way to improve the world and express generosity, but also as a *unifying force* for the whole family. *The family that gives together, lives together.* If you've developed certain habits of generosity, identified a particular cause, or established a family foundation to manage charitable giving, this section of the Family Vision Statement may urge the children to see their own philanthropic involvement as an important part of their legacy and a uniquely satisfying way for the family to cooperate for the good of others.

It's true! Charity really does begin at home. And home is the place where the greatest blessings of charity are experienced.

When my father died at the too-early age of fifty-seven, I learned yet another important and valuable lesson from him about money and giving. In the process of going through his financial documents and probating his will, I discovered several old IRS 1040 reports. What I discovered about my father was convicting. There were years his gross income was less than $3200. Yet he always gave 10 percent of his gross income (not his adjusted gross) to his local church. My wife and I (at the time) were making more than five times my father's annual income, but giving less. We were paying more on our credit cards each month than we were giving to God. We were so involved with keeping up with our friends, we had forgotten about our TRUE FRIEND. With scissors in hand and plastic in pieces, we determined to be good stewards and put God first in our finances. He has blessed that decision ever since. You will notice that our will includes a significant bequest for kingdom purposes. That's exactly how it should be . . . how we want it to be.

Step Ten: Introduction to Family Retreats and the Family Council

The Family Vision Statement is the vehicle through which you formally propose the formation of annual Family Retreats and the Family Council.

The Family Retreats—a mix of family business and family fun—will be held annually (at least) and permit your family to talk about important matters related to legacy: heritage, vision, values, philanthropy, cooperation, teamwork, listening, and leadership. They begin with the *initial* retreat—a gathering we will plan for in Chapter Nine and experience in Chapter Ten. But the intent is for these retreats to become a regular part of your family's rhythm, held every year, giving the family a chance to touch base with each other and with what really matters. If you do these retreats right with the years you have left, there is every reason to hope they will continue to be an important part of your family's life after you're gone.

The Family Council—led by a core of family members and participated in by all—is charged with overseeing, protecting, and advancing family business . . . by which we mean not the "family business" but the business of being a family. Any matter that affects the family as a whole is the responsibility of the Family Council. Some matters can be decided and determined by the leaders of the Council on behalf of the family (e.g., planning annual Family Retreats; setting the topic and agenda for each retreat; management of efforts undertaken by the family such as family foundations and philanthropic efforts). Other matters may be brought to the family as a whole for discussion of issues relevant to family health and harmony, family finances, approval of new family leadership, and so on.

Family Councils meet as often as needed, but they must meet at least once a year—called to order during the annual Family Retreats. There must be a quorum for decisions to be valid, a formal agenda, specific subjects for discussion, and free and full dialogue among family members. Since important issues are at stake, minutes of discussions should be kept and published to family members.

This final section of your Family Vision Statement gives birth to the Family Retreat and the Family Council. Read Chapter Nine and Chapter Ten to understand what you need to say to your family about these two important additions to your family's life.

Carolyn, we are asking you to serve as chair of the initial Family Council. You don't have to do this forever (a two-year term?). And you don't have to do it alone (we'll help). But this initial council is important and needs to be done well. You have the skills to shepherd this process through, the fairness to make sure the process has integrity, and a love of our family that will energize and motivate you. Thanks in advance for your willingness to lead the family in this way.

Conclusion

Congratulations! If you've done the hard work recommended in this chapter, your Family Vision Statement is coming together. We've included a checklist (230–231) in Appendix E to ensure that you have all the necessary components completed and nothing has dropped through the cracks.

Once you have all the boxes ticked, your Family Vision Statement is ready to *roll out* to your family. Notice the emphasis is on "roll out." You've put in a huge amount of work getting to this Family Vision Statement: grasping its importance, understanding the concepts behind it, putting everything on paper, making sure all the pieces are present.

But the point of all this thought and effort *is not the Family Vision Statement itself*. You are writing to be *read*. You are telling this story with an *audience* in mind. You can't do all this reflection and composing only to pack the results away, unread and fruitless! To be effective, to justify your work and achieve your legacy goals, this Family Vision Statement has to be shared with your family.

Your family may not understand everything you want to tell them. They may not be able to see the destination. Like the apostles, your family may need time to grapple with where you are leading them and why you are so determined to go there. They may balk and question and try to change the subject.

That's okay. Your family will understand eventually. Your job is to point the way. You have to step forward with a determined stride. Consider this Family Vision Statement the footprints you leave along the path to a better future.

Exercises

There are a series of exercises included in Appendix E (entitled *Chapter Eight Exercises*). These worksheets will help you write your heritage biography, personal autobiography, story of your immediate family, and so on. Samples:

- Start with general information: where your family name came from . . . your family's ethnic and national roots . . . when your ancestors came to this country . . . where they settled.
- What were you like as a teenager? Were you popular, athletic, bookish, awkward? What was your first job? Who was your first romance? What did you like to do?
- What would you identify as the three most dominant *values* that consistently run through your family (e.g., honesty, hard work, faith, open dialogue, independence, compassion)?

Note

1. Luke 13:22–31; Matthew 19:1; Mark 10:1; John 10:40.

CHAPTER NINE

PLANNING FOR LEGACY

The first thing he did was pray. Not briefly—in the hustle of the market or in snatched moments during his workaday life. Concentrated time. Dedicated time. Away from the madding crowd. Away from the routine of normal life. The wilderness. A quiet place. A private retreat.

Prayer was a regular part of the daily rhythm Jesus established. But there were particular times when Jesus dedicated significant and intensive periods to prayer: before he designated his apostles[1] . . . as he prepared to face the cross.[2]

The beginning of his ministry was such a time. After his baptism but before he began proclaiming the good news of the kingdom of heaven, Jesus devoted himself to fasting and prayer.[3]

Perhaps a day or two in the desert alone was all he intended. A respite from the normal. But the more he withdrew, the longer he stayed. Forty days was the right number. Like Noah on the flood waters. Like Moses on the mountain. Forty days to find clarity. Forty days to see his way forward. Time to hear the call. Time to know the plan.

Others would reach for a calendar, jot down the steps, lay out the process, write an agenda, make reservations. Not him. Prayer was the starting point. Prayer and fasting. A conversation between himself and God. A space for listening and communing and committing.

And when it was done, when the forty days were over, he marched from the wilderness with a confidence no one could shake. Not the crowds with their insistent demands. Not the Pharisees with their complaints and criticisms. Not Satan himself with his siren song and his easy path and his tempting, cross-less proposals.

Jesus started with prayer. And the result was a relentless, unswerving sense of mission that would not waver. Even the nails would not dissuade him. It was the nails he wanted. Praying showed him that.[4]

Planning the Future

You have traced the line of your past and seen its trajectory projected on the years ahead. You have envisioned the best future you could hope for your family—the people you love most.

Now it's time to plan.

You already have the essential building blocks of a plan in place.

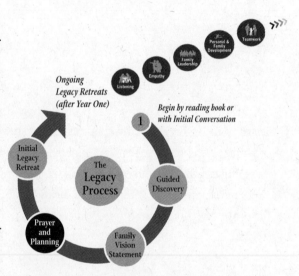

- You've thought through your *motivation* to plan for a better future. Do you want to leave your children a gift of bread or stones? Do you intend to pass on to your heirs a list of assets or a legacy? (Chapter One)
- You've *considered the odds* against a happy, healthy, long-term future for your family (the Ninety Percent Rule). And you've wrestled with the idea that faith does not exempt you from this sad prospect. (Chapter Two)

- You've asked some good *questions* and struggled to find good answers. (Chapter Three)
- You've *counted the cost* and committed to being intentional about passing on a legacy to your family, making the necessary room in your life and calendar. (Chapter Four)
- You've realized that, though the dangers of passing on possessions to your heirs are real and frightening, there is an opportunity to use your valuables to communicate and commend your *values*. (Chapter Five)
- You've accomplished the hard work of Guided Discovery and should have some practical, tangible wisdom to share with your family (stories and maxims and life lessons). (Chapter Seven)
- All of this has culminated in a Family Vision Statement that summarizes and encapsulates all the blood, sweat, and tears you've invested in developing your legacy . . . a collection of your "greatest hits" . . . a treasure chest to turn over to your loved ones. (Chapter Eight)

All that's left is to stack these building blocks into a workable plan . . . and then work the plan to the benefit of your family. Still sounds daunting, doesn't it? (It does!) Still seems like a lot of hard work, wouldn't you say? (We would!)

But you can see the finish line from here. There's your family gathered at the ribbon, urging you on, waiting to congratulate you. Or (to use a better metaphor), there are your sons and daughters waiting to run their own leg of the relay—so fresh and full of energy!—with their hands stretched out to take the legacy baton from you and continue the race into the future.

Where do you begin to formulate such a plan? For people of faith, the best-laid plans are always rooted in *prayer*. "Commit to the LORD whatever you do, and he will establish your plans" (Prov. 16:3).

Praying for an Intentional Future

In Chapter Four, we discussed the role a personal prayer commitment has in "counting the cost" of an intentional legacy. People who don't start this journey with prayer rarely make it to the finish line. We're just not that smart or strong or stubborn. We need divine help to reach the future we desire for our families.

We even suggested a prayer outline you could use in your private, daily devotions . . . a legacy prayer that would keep you focused and refreshed. We hope you've been praying that prayer. It never gets tired or rote or irrelevant.

You might want to add to that prayer outline a specific request for:

- Clarity as you make tangible plans to pass on a legacy to your progeny.
- Plans that are means to effective ends. (They don't just look good on paper, but actually accomplish what you desire.)
- Plans that are in accordance with God's higher (and often mysterious) will.
- Plans that will be embraced by your family . . . plans that will win their cooperation and collaboration.

But more than lengthening your legacy prayers, it is critical at this stage that you *widen the circle* of people who are praying this prayer with and for you. Now is the time to start praying for legacy with your *spouse*. Even if you don't pray together about anything else, this is a matter you need to pray about in concert. Your prayers will prompt not just conversation with God but dialogue with each other. They will encourage you to share your vision and hopes and dreams for the family with the person most likely to value and embrace them.

There are a few other people whose prayers (and support) will be important for you in planning for your family's future. Your minister. (Take him to Starbucks and talk about what you're doing.) One of your elders or a respected spiritual mentor. (Have them to dinner and tell them about your legacy journey.) Your parents, if they are still alive. (After all, it's their legacy, too!) Siblings? (You might want their involvement in some of your planned activities.) A trusted friend? (It will let you talk about something more substantive than sports or shopping!)

Pray deeply. And invite others to pray with you. People who love you best will be eager to pray with you about such an important matter, lifting you and your family into the presence of God on a regular basis.

The Family Retreat

Most of the specific planning outlined in this chapter relates to an initial family retreat. (We are assuming there will be subsequent annual retreats in the future.) Sooner or later, you will ask your family to gather for a "pre-inheritance" experience—a forum conducted with your family in order to focus on:

- Establishing healthy communication among family members.
- Sharing the family's story, values, and traditions.
- Talking about plans and details for the inheritance of possessions.
- Unveiling and discussing the Family Vision Statement.
- Encouraging family members to experience a Guided Discovery of their own.
- Organizing a structure for future family unity (the Family Council).
- Preparing heirs to receive valuables without undermining their values.
- Passing leadership to the next generation.

The retreat can be held at a hotel, conference center, family vacation home, destination resort—anywhere the family will have the opportunity to work together in comfortable surroundings. It will involve a formal agenda, cover specific family business, and require participation from family members. (Fun, by the way, should always be an important part of the retreat mix.)

Some parents simply call their children and grandchildren. Others prepare and mail official invitations. However family members are invited, the idea for the retreat is the same: to provide an opportunity to strengthen family commitments, implement a family council structure, broaden the family leadership base, and pass on family values. If everyone doesn't show up for the retreat, you can work with those who do.

The planning you'll do in this chapter relates to the initial Family Retreat. In the next chapter, we'll talk about this retreat in more detail—paint a picture and give examples of the way the retreat works. It might help you formulate a better plan if you "begin with the end in mind" and read the next chapter so you have a clear understanding of what you are hoping to accomplish.

Who, When, Where, and How

Planning a Family Retreat starts by answering the "Who?" question. Who should be invited? Who needs to be sitting at the table for an effective Family Retreat to take place?

- You and your spouse.
- Your children and their spouses.
- Grandchildren. (Since the business of this retreat requires participants who have the patience and processing ability to learn and contribute, you might want to provide a sitter for younger grandchildren during those parts of the retreat that require the adults to give their full attention to legacy matters.)
- A facilitator to lead discussions and keep the agenda moving along, if desired.

Remember, this Family Retreat isn't about lectures and presentations. Passing on *information* is not the most important thing your family will do at a retreat. The greatest opportunity afforded by a retreat involves dialogue and sharing and authentic interaction.

Now, think about *when*. We are all busy people. Coordinating schedules, saving the date, and clearing calendars to be fully "present" at the retreat can be a challenge. Is your family more available for a weekend retreat? Do logistics (e.g., travel, distance, location) recommend setting aside a longer period of time?

We suggest you schedule at least a day and a half for the Family Retreat. *Any less* won't let you make the progress toward legacy that justifies your investment of time and resources. *Any more* will wear family members out and threaten the family's willingness to commit to future retreats. If you want to begin and end with additional days of fun, togetherness, and relaxation, that's up to you. (It's always a good idea, however.)

What is important at this point is that you nail down specific dates for the Family Retreat. That may require a few "calendar conversations" with your kids. You could offer a couple of options about the timing of the retreat. Even then, the precise dates will remain a moving target. But, for purposes of invitation and dialogue, you need some recommended dates as a starting point.

Where? As in real estate, successful retreats depend on *location, location, location*. Finding a venue that is comfortable, accessible, quiet, and private can be difficult. Choose a site that is *too near* the normal lives of your family, and you'll have a hard time convincing everyone to drop the urgent to concentrate on the important. *Too remote*, and the more time and money you'll spend just getting there and back. Be realistic. Make necessary compromises. But keep the point of the retreat in mind and make sure the place fits the purpose.

Finally, *how?* The devil, as they say, is in the details. Good planning accounts for logistics and realities. Here are just a few of the particulars you should consider.

- Travel arrangements and expenses
- Your budget
- Meals and housing
- Gathering room (quiet, private, comfortable)
- Refreshments
- Child care needs
- Equipment (e.g., video projector, screen, laptop, camcorder, connections)

Defining the What and the Why

Everything else you're doing in this chapter—all the logistics and calendar arrangements and documents and invitations—supports the *what* and the *why* of your Family Retreat.

The *why*, of course, is legacy . . . the family's future . . . the sad reality of the Ninety Percent Rule . . . your higher hopes for those you love. Much of this book is about the *why*. If you hadn't tumbled to that by now . . . well, you wouldn't still be reading.

The *what* comes down to an agenda—a tangible discussion plan covering specific items for particular periods of time. Chapter Ten will present more details about the Family Retreat and its agenda. For now, keep the following key points in mind for planning purposes:

- Introducing the purpose of the Family Retreat.
- Having a "pre-inheritance" discussion.
- Explaining the difference between valuables and values.
- Sharing the family story (heritage).
- Sharing your personal story (testimony).
- Experiencing Guided Discovery as a family.
- Unveiling the Family Vision Statement.
- Setting up the Family Council.
- Planning for the next Family Retreat.

Gathering Your Documents

If you have done more than *read* this book—if you've actually done the exercises found at the close of most chapters and invested the work in creating a Family Vision Statement, you have a significant stack of written notes at your fingertips . . . the nuts and bolts from which your family can build the vehicle to carry them into the future.

Let's review the documents you should have collected and composed over the course of your legacy journey. The *Planning Documents Checklist* (233–234) is provided in Appendix F. If you've already gathered these notes and documents in a journal or loose-leaf binder, you can skip this step. Just make sure you've got all your work in one place. How sad to have gone to all this effort only to have a significant scrap slip through the cracks and get lost in the avalanche of paper your heirs will wade through when you are gone!

Make sure these documents are readily available and that you've made copies for each of your heirs (as appropriate).

Sneak Preview

Everybody needs context.

One of the best things you can do to prepare your heirs for the future is to prepare them for the initial Family Retreat. To be prepared, they need a context. Don't let the first notice your family receives about the Family Retreat be an invitation in the mail. Drop some hints. Mention your legacy journey. Take them for coffee and recount a story about the family you've just uncovered.

Have an "off the cuff" conversation about the meaning of family. Ask them some of the same questions you've been asking yourself.

You need your family to know what the Family Retreat is about, why it is important, why their participation is so necessary, what you hope to accomplish. You'll tell them all that at the retreat itself, of course. But a sneak peak at the *what* and the *why* will help them put the retreat in a wider context. It will show them the reason their "yes" is so vital to you.

An invitation to join in the legacy prayer might be your excuse to mention (by the way) your hopes for hosting a Family Retreat in the near future. A quick question about schedules over the next few months might be just the opening you need to introduce the retreat idea.

Or, perhaps, a request for help might be just the ticket!

Broadening Participation

We've already assured you that you don't have to do all this alone. And we've mentioned the availability of facilitators who have the experience and skills to help you through the legacy process.

But there is another source of partnership we should mention: members of your family. One of the best ways to ensure active participation in the Family Retreat is to invite active partnership in preparing for it. There are any number of ways a son or daughter, a grandchild, or a son- or daughter-in-law could help with preparations for the Family Retreat, such as:

- Collecting and copying documents.
- Proofreading your Family Vision Statement.
- Finding good venue options for the Family Retreat.
- Coordinating schedules to determine a date.
- Preparing PowerPoint presentations about the family's past.
- Making meal reservations or providing refreshments.
- Organizing child care.
- Sending out invitations and managing RSVPs.
- Helping you write a readable personal testimonial.

Few things are more powerful than telling members of your family that you *need* them . . . and then inviting them to *help* you achieve significant goals through significant contributions. By asking for help, you are increasing the probabilities of a successful Family Retreat before the retreat even begins.

The "Ask"

So . . . you're praying. You've gathered all your documents. You've raised the retreat idea with different family members at different times. You've found a place and set a date. A daughter is gathering family pictures so her husband can put together a PowerPoint presentation. A grandkid is looking into child care options.

It's *invitation* time.

An invitation to a Family Retreat is important and deserves some careful thought. It doesn't have to be expensively engraved or printed on fancy paper. But it is far more than a "save the date" notice to hang from the refrigerator door. Yes, it must contain details like *where* and *when*. But, more, it must also communicate:

- The importance of this retreat (to you personally and to the family's future).
- Your expectations about the family's attendance and participation.
- A promise that—at the retreat—the family will be talking about their inheritance and the larger-than-money legacy you want to leave them.
- A request that they make the retreat a personal priority, arrange to be there the entire time (no late arrivals or early exits), and commit to being fully "present" in body, mind, and spirit.

That's a lot to ask of one piece of paper. But it's also a lot to ask of the members of your family. A little time and creativity, a little thought and prayer, will go a long way as you prepare to invite the people you love to participate in a retreat that will focus on the future of the family they share.

Conclusion

What began for Jesus as *prayer* resulted in a *plan* that guided him through the rest of his life. We don't know whether God delivered the plan to Jesus fully formed and richly detailed, or showed him the big picture and expected him to fill in the details. But we do know that God intended Jesus to walk a certain path and promised to walk beside him on the journey.

In a similar way, you may not know how the plan for your legacy and your family's future will be revealed to you by your Father. Maybe God will drop a phone-book-sized proposal on your head. Maybe (more likely) he'll lift you high enough to see over the horizon and then trust you to chart an intentional course.

What we know for sure is this: so long as we commit our ways to him, he will establish our plans. And that is why the best-laid plans—every single one of them—start with prayer.

Exercise

In Appendix F, you will find a list of planning documents that you need to complete and collect, including:

- Legal documents (such as your will).
- Your notes on the exercises of previous chapters.
- Letters you've written to future generations.
- Your Family Vision Statement.

Notes

1. Luke 6:12–15.
2. Mark 14:32–36.
3. Mark 1:9–13.
4. John 12:27.

CHAPTER TEN

THE FAMILY RETREAT

> *With many similar parables Jesus spoke the word to them,*
> *as much as they could understand. He did not say anything*
> *to them without using a parable.*
> *(Mark 4:33–34)*

He told them parables because they could not take the truth full strength. They needed small portions at a time, diluted with candied sweets and pretty colors.

He told them parables because, even when they grasped the truth, they let it flitter away so quickly. The parables were the barbs he carved into truth to help it stick in the hearts of his hearers.

But mostly he told them parables because the people loved stories. They would listen in rapt attention while he painted word pictures of coins lost and found, greedy managers, wandering sons, and seed-sowing farmers. The parables were poetry in a desert of prose. People panted for them.

Jesus was a storyteller par excellence. He believed in the power of stories. Stories were his favored method for teaching the crowds and engaging his listeners. He could have conveyed truth through cold propositional statements arranged into alphabetized lists. He could have treated truth like it was algebra or chemistry.

Instead, he told parables.[1]

Try this little exercise: Ask a few people what beatitude comes after "Blessed are the meek." (Bet they won't know.) Ask them to recite a teaching of Jesus about fasting . . . or prayer . . . or tithing. (They may give you a blank look.) Then ask them to finish the parable that begins: "Once there was a man who had two sons. The younger son said to his father . . ." (You'll be amazed at the detail they recall.)

So, if parables are so powerful, if stories are so compelling and memorable, why don't you and I tell more tales to those we love most?

The Family Retreat

Imagine you and your spouse, your children and their spouses, and even grown grandchildren (if you have them) all meeting in the same room, at the same time, to discuss the past and future of your family . . . the valuables and values that comprise your family's "treasure."

What do you see in your mind's eye? An edifying experience in harmony and cooperation? Or fingernails clawed slowly down a chalkboard, a riot ready to erupt? Or (worse yet!) an outbreak of boredom and barely suppressed yawns?

Your family might be able to pull off a multi-day discussion of values, vision, the family's money, and the family's future without a hitch. Congratulations! Lucky you!

But for many families, all those related people gathered in the same room with all their baggage (the emotional, not the suitcase, variety!) will likely lead to . . . well . . . *interesting* results. Take a few children and stepchildren, sprinkle in a couple of sullen teenagers, and mix them together with hard realities like siblings who haven't spoken to each other for years . . . and the combination can be explosive. It's enough to remind you of nuclear blasts or hurricanes or long falls off high cliffs.

The idea of family Armageddon rather than family bliss may not strike you as the most uplifting or promising way to introduce the idea of a Family Retreat (the next step in the Legacy Process). But the Legacy Process is not an abstract philosophical ideal. It is designed and intended to work in the real world. And in the real world, families have unique and often turbulent histories, filled with equal measures of joy and accomplishment, sorrow and pain.

The bad news is that there are no perfect or perfectly functioning families. There are only families (like yours and mine) with their share of failings and foibles.

The good news is that even imperfect and flawed families (like yours and mine) can gather to talk productively about matters that matter. All you need is something "worth talking about" (like a Family Vision Statement—see Chapter Eight), a plan to create a "talking opportunity" (which you laid out in Chapter Nine), and a structure that encourages "honest and respectful talking" (the retreat we'll discuss in the present chapter).

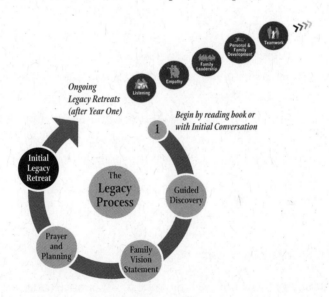

Families that want to be healthy, families that want to pass on a legacy, *meet*. Good communication takes *practice*. Talking about matters that matter in your family involves *time*. Working through family issues requires *focus* and *deliberation* and *interaction*.

And these meetings have to be more than casual get-togethers without form or structure or agenda. There is a level of intentionality needed to transform "family time" into "legacy time."

That's what Family Retreats are about. They are opportunities for families to come together, connect with each other, and focus *on the business of being a family.* Don't think of Family Retreats as a one-shot effort, accomplished in a grueling marathon of meeting-endurance, done once and then never again. Think more of a series of family "workouts," leisurely and fun, experienced together on a regular basis, slowly leading to a healthier and heartier family.

We recommend your family set aside some time every year (a couple of days?) to focus on the family, talk about your family's legacy, tell stories from the family's past, and prepare for the family's future (by discussing matters such as leadership, teamwork, listening, etc.).

The initial Family Retreat, the one that kicks off future retreats and sets the tone for the family time to come, is critical to the ongoing success of these meetings. Do the initial retreat well, and your family will begin to anticipate and celebrate subsequent retreats. But the retreats to follow are also important. They allow the family to build on the foundation you will lay together at that first retreat.

Perhaps a bit of definition would be helpful at this juncture. Family Retreats are the more formal version of something you've probably already experienced: the family reunion. The Family Retreat can be defined as:

> A gathering of family members for the purpose of communicating about family matters, implementing a family structure, broadening the family leadership base, strengthening family commitments, and passing on family values.

The structure of the Family Retreat boils down to an agenda that not only establishes certain topics to talk about (like the Ninety Percent Rule and Guided Discovery) but also establishes certain rules and guidelines to follow as the family talks (e.g., only one speaker at a time). Most of all, this structure encourages the telling of stories that have meaning for and interest to the family . . . stories that are *about* the family, stories that convey family values and family history.

These stories carry your family "truths." They are the barbs that make the truths stick. And you will be amazed at how powerful, how compelling and memorable, these stories will prove to be for the members of your family. They'll hang on every word.

The Initial Family Retreat Agenda

We've already spent some time thinking through and planning for the initial Family Retreat. (See Chapter Nine.) We've walked through many of the logistics for this first retreat and thought carefully about communicating its purpose and goals.

Now we're ready to write a script for the retreat . . . to decide where we need to start and where we want to end and what will be said betwixt and between. The basic outline (for a one-day retreat) looks like this:

	Topic	Saturday Schedule
1.	Welcome and expression of affection	9:00–9:10
2.	Introducing purpose of Family Retreats	9:10–9:20
3.	Pre-inheritance discussion (valuables and values)	9:20–9:45
4.	Telling the family story (heritage)	9:45–10:30
	Coffee Break	**10:30–11:00**
5.	Telling your personal story (testimony)	11:00–12:00
6.	Unveiling the Family Vision Statement	12:00–12:15
	Lunch Break	**12:15–1:30**
7.	Experiencing Guided Discovery as a family	1:30–2:30
8.	Exercise/activity on family communication	2:30–3:00
9.	Setting up the Family Council	3:00–3:30
10.	Overview of ongoing retreats	3:30–4:00

Let's take each of these items and flesh them out, imagine them more fully, and think about what needs to be accomplished with each step.

Welcome and Expression of Affection

Can you see it? Your entire family is together in one room. Half of them are gathered around the coffeepot, eating donuts and laughing. Some are off in corners, in pairs or trios, engaged in earnest conversation. A few keep to themselves, headphones plugged in or nose stuck in a book.

It's 9:05 on a Saturday morning—past time to begin. You clear your throat and call for everyone's attention. If your family is like mine, no one pays any heed; they keep right on talking. So you raise your volume a bit and try again. Your oldest daughter hears and adds her voice (louder and shriller!) to yours: "HEY EVERYBODY! IT'S TIME TO START!"

You ask everyone to find a seat (there are comfortable couches arranged around a love seat and a projection screen). You and your spouse sit in the love seat. The kids grab one last donut or put away their iPads and move to the couches. They sit and look to you with expectant expressions.

You've anticipated this moment for months. You've worked hard to prepare for this family gathering. You have high hopes for what your family is about to experience and accomplish together. And you know exactly what you want your first words to be.

> Welcome, everyone. Thank you for saving the time and making the effort to be here for our initial Family Retreat. Your presence and participation mean the world to us.
>
> In fact, you mean the world to us . . . period. You are the most important people in our lives . . . without exception. This family means more to us than we can express. We're not perfect—as a family or as individuals. We've had our ups and downs together. But it's that last word—"together"—that means so much. We are a family. That means we walk through life together. No matter what may come, no matter how hard things get, no matter what changes, our greatest hope is that this family can stay together, play together, and work together as a family.
>
> That's what this retreat is all about.

Ten pairs of eyes are fixed on you. Your spouse holds your hand and squeezes encouragement. Your daughter and her husband and their eighteen-year-old son sit on one couch. On the couch next to them—crowded together—sits your middle son (starting to gray at the temples . . . when did that happen?) with his wife and their newly married daughter clinging proudly to her fresh-faced husband. On the third couch is your never-married son (the one with

"All who wander are not lost" tattooed on his shoulder) and his tall, lanky, twenty-one-year-old nephew—the first child of your daughter.

This is your family. These are the people for whom you have worked so hard over the years. These are the ones who will carry your legacy into the future.

Introducing the Purpose of the Family Retreat

You take a deep breath. You say a quick prayer. And then you plunge ahead.

> We've been looking forward to this retreat for months. And we've worked hard for months to make our time together something we can enjoy and that will bless this family for years to come.
>
> And, whether you realize it or not, you have also been preparing for this retreat—your whole life! You've been an important part of defining and shaping who we are as a family, what we do together, what we think is important, how we treat each other. The things we'll talk about this weekend belong to you.
>
> There are other people in the room who have made preparation for this retreat as well. You can't see them. They aren't present physically. Some are long dead. They are our "larger" family, our ancestors, the ones who plowed the ground and sowed the seed for the family we are today. We want to recognize the contribution past family members have made to our character and values and history together. We'll talk about when family traditions got started. We'll tell the stories that have shaped the DNA of our life together as a family.
>
> This retreat is all about legacy, an inheritance that has been passed on to us by the ancestors who bore our family name two hundred years ago. By your great-great-great-grandmother (you nod at your oldest grandson) who immigrated to this country with nothing more than a suitcase and a dream. By my grandfather who became a pastor and gave us a great legacy of faith. By your grandmother (you nod to your spouse) who started our family business.

> We have a wonderful family with deep roots and deep values
> and deep commitments. This retreat is about hearing family
> stories and affirming family traits and celebrating our family's
> legacy.

Your eyes shine as you survey the precious people around you. You feel overwhelmed by your love for them, your gratitude for those who have gone before, and the powerful legacy your ancestors gave to you and that now—in turn—you get to pass on to your children.

A "Pre-Inheritance" Discussion

You swallow. You offer a quick prayer of gratitude. And then you jump in again.

> When I use the word "legacy," I mean there is more to our family
> than stuff. We are not defined by assets and portfolios and
> properties. There is more to us than our material possessions. So,
> if I were to ask you what it means to belong to this family, to wear
> our family name, what would you say?

You pause and look around at your loved ones. They look blankly at you . . . as though you have posed a question they don't quite understand. You wait. You give them time to consider. You let the conversation breathe.

Your eldest, the daughter, jumps in eventually. She was always the bold one. "Our family knows how to work hard!" She says it with conviction but still looks at you with the question, "Is that what you meant?" in her eyes.

"That's true. Members of our family have never been afraid of hard work," you assure her.

"For me," your oldest son speaks up, "our best quality as a family is that we make room for other people. When we were growing up, there was always a willingness to set another plate at the table, for friends to come over, for people to stay in the guest room." He thought for a moment and then added, "I saw Grandma doing that all the time. I bet we learned it from her."

Heads nod all around—remembering.

And then your granddaughter's new husband asks, "Can I say something?" He swallows and then plunges on. "I've been amazed at how comfortable you are getting into each other's business!"

Everyone laughs (a little nervously). They know exactly what he's talking about. It's a family joke: not being very good at boundaries.

"I mean, in my family, we didn't get too personal. We didn't talk about private things. But you guys," he smiles to show he's not being critical, "you stick your nose right in and ask questions and give advice. You seem . . . " He swallowed again. "You seem to trust each other enough to risk getting personal."

His young wife pats his knee. "It can be a bit overwhelming," she sympathized.

"It can!" he agrees. "But I like it." He smiles again and adds, "Most of the time."

You let the give-and-take go on for several minutes. The characteristics and qualities that are mentioned are just the sort of family traits you wanted to come up. They are the perfect setup for what you'd like to discuss next.

> I don't want to get morbid, but one day we will be gone (you give your spouse's hand a squeeze). And everything we have, everything we are, will go to you.
>
> Yes, we have a will and each of you should expect to receive a material inheritance from us. It is a joy for us to pass an inheritance to you. We want to talk about the details of that soon.
>
> But, in a very real sense, you have already received your most important inheritance from us—the legacy of our family. It's the qualities you've just been talking about, the values we share, the lessons you've learned from your grandparents, the faith that is growing in each of you. Nothing we could give you, no material asset, would be as valuable as that legacy. Without the legacy, the assets mean nothing. In fact, apart from the legacy, the assets will prove a curse rather than a blessing.
>
> Do you know what the Ninety Percent Rule is?

Tell them what happens when families pass on possessions without emphasizing principles. Let them know the odds against succeeding. (Review Chapter Two.) Sharing this statistic with your family is not a scare tactic; it is a sobering truth. Your heirs need to know that your valuables are the least valuable thing they will receive from you. They need to understand that the future of the family's health, harmony, and happiness depends far less on the quantity of the assets they inherit than on the quality of the legacy they receive.

> The money is the easy part. It's the meaning that's difficult. What good is it, really, to pass on possessions without passing on the ethics that produced them, the attitudes that managed them, or the priorities that determined how they were utilized? So what if you inherit the world from us; if you lose your souls as a result, where's the profit in that? (quote from Chapter Two)

Let them process this for a few moments. Do they understand the difficulties? Do they see the dangers? Assure them you have higher hopes for them . . . and a plan to help your family become a Ten Percent Family.

At this point, pass out the agenda for the initial Family Retreat (you'll find it a few pages back) and summarize what the family will be doing over the next few hours.

Telling the Family Story (Heritage)

Once your family has learned the reasons for the Family Retreat and the challenges before them, it's time for a treat: stories!

In Chapter Seven (*Your Guided Discovery*), you did most of the work that goes into sharing the story of the family heritage with your family. You learned that, in order to go forward, it is important for your family to go back . . . to remember where you came from and who planted and nourished your characteristic family traits. The past is a quarry containing all the treasures your present family requires to build a solid foundation for the future.

You've put together a family tree. You've learned the names of ancestors. You've gathered photos and important documents. You've collected stories (the "founding" narratives) that have shaped your family, formed its core character, and demonstrated its strengths and values. (It's OK if you don't have *everything* finished, bound, and perfectly formatted. The most important thing you have to share is something you've been preparing your entire life: your story, your values, your vision.)

If you completed the work of Chapter Eight (*Your Vision Statement*—especially the biography exercise), you wrote a memoir about your extended family—a chronicle of your family history. You've put your heritage into a form that allows you to tell your family about their own past. They'll love the story! Who doesn't want to hear stories about themselves?

If you followed the suggestion in Chapter Nine (*Planning for Legacy*), you have asked one of your tech-savvy offspring to prepare a PowerPoint presentation—all those photos and birth certificates and incorporation papers and maps in full color and HD graphics!

So dim the lights, fire up the laptop, and run through that story now. No need to rush—let everyone enjoy the tale. But, on the other hand, don't dawdle. You're telling a story, but you don't have to tell the *whole* story, with every twist and turn, dwelling on every excruciating detail. Future Family Retreats will give you the chance to unpack the story more completely. The goal of *this* version of the family story is to tell something that is clear and compelling, that introduces the personalities and themes inspiring your family, and that recounts the "founding narratives" defining the essence of your family's soul.

We thought you might enjoy an example of the sort of family story that can capture a family's heart.

This is a picture of my maternal grandmother. We called her Granny. (I know. Not very imaginative, but . . .) The picture was taken in 1943—during the awful days of World War II. She's still young here . . . in her early thirties. But, by this time, she's had all five of her children. And, by this time, she has resigned herself to the hard fact that her husband was a drunk and a philanderer and a poor provider for the family.

To feed and house her children, she worked as a kindergarten teacher and a department store salesperson, and she took in sewing jobs on the side. Soon after this picture was taken, she went to work for Sears Roebuck—designing and sewing draperies. She worked very hard at her job, at raising her children, at being a good person. She never had much money. But she always had time for people and room in her heart for the hurting.

Church was important to Granny. My Mom tells stories of Granny getting the kids up early on Sunday mornings, scrubbing their faces and dressing them, then walking to the train tracks to flag down a locomotive on its way into town. There was a mile walk at the other end—from the nearest stop to the church building— and Granny would make the trek like a goose leading her goslings to living water. She did this for years—until she could finally afford a car to make the drive. And she did it alone—without the help (and often despite the interference) of her wandering husband.

Granny was not "great" in the way that word is often defined. She didn't invent any gadgets. She wasn't a leader or a speaker. She never made much money. But here is her legacy to me . . . to us. Over the past thirty years, I've met scores of people who knew my grandmother—most of them people she went to church with. She taught one desperate woman to sew and found her a job at Sears. She brought others into her home and shared her meager table. She took time to listen to people and share their troubles. She had a rare combination of competence and kindness. She radiated "heart with a spine": the confidence that people can overcome their problems and the compassion to help them do so.

Every person I ever met who knew my grandmother loved me because they loved her. I grew in their eyes because my grandmother was such a giant. They showed me kindness because they had received kindness from her. They treated me generously because that is how she had treated them. It's been over thirty years since her death, and I still meet people who want me to know how much my grandmother meant to them.

Legacy? Here's a legacy. No matter how hard things get, do the right thing. No matter how mistreated you are, treat others with kindness and compassion. No matter what life brings, never feel sorry for yourself or surrender to self-pity. No matter how lonely you feel, always remember that God is present and can be counted on for grace and strength. That's a legacy I wouldn't trade for all the gold in Fort Knox.

This would be a good time for a short coffee break . . . a few minutes for these "first things first" principles to sink in: the purpose of the Family Retreat, the distinction between valuables and values, the central place of "legacy" in what you want to share with those you love best, and the way stories of the past shape the present and future.

Another donut, another cup of coffee, will help these enduring ideas digest more easily.

Telling Your Personal Story (Testimonial)

Once your *general* family story is told, it's time for you and your spouse to tell your *specific and personal* stories . . . two stories that have become one story . . . one story that is often the most powerful, poignant part of the Family Retreat.

Without theatrics or gimmicks, Mom and Dad simply sit in front of their children (and grandchildren) and tell about their childhood and teen years, their formative influences, how they met and married, the early married years, the birth of children, where the family lived, their career paths, and so on.

In Chapter Seven, you did most of the work that goes into sharing your personal story with your family. You've gathered photos and important documents (wedding pictures, places your family has lived, birth certificates, etc.). You've collected tales (such as favorite memories of your marriage and the kids, important decisions and commitments you and your spouse made, traditions your family has honored together, times of challenge and success). You've reflected on the people, principles, and priorities that have influenced your immediate family. All that now becomes a smorgasbord from which you can select the memory meal that will nourish your family's legend and legacy.

If you completed the work of Chapter Eight—especially the exercise *Our Family Story*—you wrote a memoir about your personal life and the life of your immediate family. You've put your testimonial into a form that allows you to tell your family about your own life and theirs.

You may have organized all this into a PowerPoint presentation. If so, it will help you tell this story in an orderly, visual manner. But PowerPoint is not the point. A handful of photos, a handwritten outline, will let you tell your story just as well. The important thing is for you to gather the narrative of your life and family into a single telling, look your family in the eye (and allow them to look into your heart), and pass on that precious story to the people you love.

These very intimate stories always contain elements that surprise the listeners. Your story will fill in the blank spaces between the parts the family already knows. (In our experience, those blank spaces—for many families—are quite substantial.) Your children will learn things about your childhood, your awkward teenage years, your courtship and early marriage that they have never heard before. It can be difficult for young adults or teenage children who have known nothing but the privileged life of suburban America to comprehend when Mom talks about sewing patches on Dad's work jeans ("Dad wore jeans? Dad got his hands dirty?"), or picking fruit to can for lean winters, or dinners of pork and beans. Tales of one-room apartments, cars that should have gone to the junkyard but were kept alive one more month, early business failures, banks refusing loans, partnerships that crumbled—sacrifice after hardscrabble sacrifice—often bring the toughest entrepreneurs to tears and almost always leave their children with a new measure of respect for their parents . . . and a renewed appreciation of how God sustains and provides for those who love him.

Here are a few of the responses you're likely to get when you tell your story: *"I had no idea it was that hard for you"*; *"Life was so different when you were our age"*; *"It's amazing that one idea* [or opportunity or chance encounter or event] *can have such an impact for so long and for so many people."* In fact, even as you tell your story, the questions from your family might come so thick and fast that you have to ask them to reserve their queries just so you can get to the end! One thing is certain: they will be riveted; they'll soak up the story like sponges; they'll hear you out with a greater appreciation for and a deeper understanding of you, the family, and themselves.

Unveiling the Family Vision Statement

After you've finished telling your specific and personal story, you should have copies of the Family Vision Statement on hand to give each member of your family. Pass them out now.

You've poured a great deal of work into this statement. You've researched, reflected on, and recorded your most cherished memories and insights. You have attempted to make your dreams for your family *clear* and *compelling*.

Now, your task is to help your family embrace this vision, adopt it, and claim it as family "common ground." If you remember the challenge presented in Chapter Eight:

> In the end, "your" vision must become "our" vision. What begins
> as a private vision must morph into a vision held in common. A
> vision that is not embraced and adopted by your family is no more
> than a personal dream—good only for as long as you draw breath.
> Until it is owned by your children and grandchildren, your vision
> for your family is just words and aspirations, not the practical
> guide you need to help your family navigate the future.

The document you distribute to your heirs may *look* finished. It may be beautifully formatted and expensively bound. The packaging *ought* to reflect the work you've invested and the importance you place on this statement.

But don't let the cover define the book. This is not a *completed* document. Consider it Version 1.0—a beta version designed to put your initial efforts into the hands of those who will actually *use* it to build the future. In order for this Family Vision Statement to become the *family's,* it will require the family's consideration, editing, correction, and acceptance. Ultimately, this statement must be a multi-authored project.

So as you hand out copies of the Family Vision Statement to your loved ones, make it clear that their participation in the final version is necessary. Here's how you and your spouse might begin:

Our family is on an exciting journey. We've come a long way from the days of our ancestors. But there is a long path ahead of us. We need to understand where we're going. We need to be united in getting there. We need to be ready to stay the course when times get tough.

Let us read you something:

"Vision is critical for families. Families perish for lack of vision. Not for lack of trying or lack of resources or lack of good intentions. Lack of vision. Families without vision bumble into the future without guidance or direction. They 'make it up' as they go along. They take any road. They follow the path of least resistance.

"Vision steers. It inspires. It leads. In the best of times, vision lets us stride forward with confidence because we know where we are going. In the tough times, when our way gets confused and the path peters out, vision helps us stay the course and persist through difficulties. Without vision—clear, compelling, common vision— our family won't walk in the right direction . . . we'll stop when we should keep going . . . we won't stay together for the duration of the journey" [quoted from Chapter Eight].

We believe that. We believe a clear, compelling, and common vision is critical to our family and its future. This document [hold up the Family Vision Statement] is our attempt to put our family vision into words. We've tried to describe our family, tell its story, identify our central values and most cherished traditions. We've written about the things that matter to us, our highest hopes and best dreams for you and for tomorrow.

And now, we are putting this in your hands and asking you to take the baton for the next leg of our journey. Read it. Think about it. Pray over it. What would you add? What do you agree or disagree with? What would it take to turn this into a document you could embrace as a road map to our family's future . . . a map you could recommend to your children and grandchildren?

We [nod at your spouse] want to talk to each of you over the coming months about your reactions to this statement. We are eager to see your edits and hear your suggestions. Our next Family Retreat will focus on your thoughts about this statement: how it can be improved . . . what you consider to be the core of this family.

In the end, I hope we can come up with a document that all of us can be excited about, something we can pass on to next generations, something that will guide us in the short term and inspire us for the long haul.

Any questions or comments?

After you've responded to any queries or remarks, another break would be appropriate at this point. Talking about family stories and family goals can be engrossing, emotional, and exhausting. Your listeners will need a rest after thinking through such heavy matters. *You* will need a rest!

Eat lunch. Take a power nap. Go for a walk in the woods. Refresh. Replenish. Restore. Get yourself (get your family!) in a position to finish the day productively.

Experiencing Guided Discovery as a Family

You had an opportunity to go through a Guided Discovery on your own or with your spouse. Whether your "guide" was this book or a facilitator, you had an opportunity to explore some very important themes about your heritage, immediate family, faith, and goals.

It is not enough for you to deliver the *results* of your Guided Discovery to the members of your family—they need to experience the process for themselves. Of course, it probably took you several hours (perhaps several days or weeks!) to work through the Guided Discovery process. You won't have time during the retreat to give your heirs the same experience. But you can give them a *sample* and encourage your family to do the hard but rewarding work of going "back to the future."

As you gather again following the lunch break, introduce the Guided Discovery process to everyone. If you have a facilitator present, this would be a good time to turn proceedings over to him or her. Let the facilitator give your family a sample of the same process you went through. She or he will probably have a short questionnaire for the family to fill out and will then conduct a group interview with the children (on the basis of their answers).

The facilitator will help keep the discussion moving but also provide a secure, supportive, and productive environment. Family members must feel safe and confident if they are to participate in this discussion fully and honestly.

If, on the other hand, you are leading this discussion yourself, the following outline might be helpful.

1. Give each member of your family a copy of this book (*Leaving a Legacy*). Tell them how helpful the book has been for you (we hope it *has* been helpful!) and point them to Chapter Seven particularly—*Your Guided Discovery*.
2. Testify to the importance of this process to your own journey of discovery and your conclusions about the importance of legacy to the family as a whole.
3. Go over the Legacy Matrix with them and talk about the various influences that make up your family's legacy: Heritage, Life Lessons, Mentors, and so on.
4. Encourage them to work through the questions and exercises in this chapter to develop their own understanding of and appreciation for the family's legacy.
5. Then give them a sampling of what they will experience. We'd suggest focusing on 1) the story of your immediate family, and 2) the character traits that form the core of being a member of this family. These are facets of the Guided Discovery that family members know well, have opinions about, and can speak to confidently.

The following are a few questions you might explore together for an hour or so.

Immediate Family Questions
- What are your first memories of our family?
- What are your most significant memories of our family? What do you value about those memories?
- What are the traditions we've observed as a family that mean the most to you? What meaning do those particular traditions hold for you?

- What was the most surprising new thing you learned about our family as we [the parents] were sharing our testimonials this morning?
- On a scale of one to ten, where do relationships with members of your immediate family rate in your life?

Family Trait Questions

- Hand out the My Character exercise from Appendix D and ask your family to identify their most defining personal characteristics.
- Which of these character traits would you identify as most characteristic of the family as a whole?

Whether a facilitator leads the discussion or you do the honors, creating a secure, supportive, and productive environment is vital. Overwhelming your family with questions and recording detailed responses is not the point of this exercise. The *point* is to encourage family members to share memories, reflect on family traits, and begin to recognize the legacy they have already inherited. To do this, they must feel safe, affirmed, and curious.

This brief Guided Discovery exercise, of course, is only a beginning, a taste, of a more intensive process. Your heirs should be encouraged to take this experience to another level, a more personal level. Challenge them to read the book and apply the Guided Discovery process to themselves. You may even plan for a facilitator to be present at your next Family Retreat to guide the family into a deeper awareness of legacy and a deeper appreciation of the true treasure of your family.

Exercises and Activities about Family Communication

Like everything else you try to excel in, good communication requires practice, practice, practice. Listening is hard. Staying on topic is tough. Sharing personal, intimate stuff is difficult.

Communicating within families poses real challenges. There are bad habits to overcome, history to step over, personalities to accommodate. But nothing constructive happens in families without *good* communication . . .

healthy, productive, and affirming communication. All families can learn to communicate better. But it takes practice!

There are many activities and exercises that help a family *practice* communication. Books have been written on the subject. Entire websites are dedicated to this matter. Whatever techniques and methods you identify, it is important that *every* Family Retreat address the need for and practice the skills of good communication.

One of the exercises we find productive for families is to hold up an empty shoebox. Say:

> This shoebox represents our family. All the good and bad. The
> positive and negative. The stuff we're proud of . . . the stuff we'd
> rather forget. If you could identify one thing, one habit or attitude
> or characteristic you see in our family, that you appreciate most
> and believe will help our family move forward to its best future,
> what would it be?

And then pass the box around. Have each family member put something into the box . . . something good and positive and healthy they already see in the family (or hope to see) . . . talk about it and what it means to them . . . and then place it (lovingly) into the box.

Once everyone has had a chance to affirm some nourishing qualities about the family, hold the box up, pray over it, and thank God for putting such blessings into the heart of your family.

Then hold up the box again for all to see.

> No family is perfect, including ours. There is stuff in our family—
> habits, attitudes, characteristics—that is getting in the way of our
> best future. If you could take one thing out of our family, what
> would it be?

Then pass the box back around. Have each family member reach into the box . . . pull out something they believe is holding the family back . . . talk about it and how it causes harm . . . and then (symbolically) throw it away. It is important, during this phase of the exercise, for individuals not to get critical or caustic, not to judge or accuse. And it is important for the rest of the family to listen, not rebut.

Just a simple little exercise. A cheap visual aid and a few instructions. But you'll be amazed at the conversation that results, the emotions expressed, the suggestions made. Your family will communicate about family. And that is a rare and precious thing.

Setting Up the Family Council

The principal vehicle for the discussion and management of the "business of being a family" (as defined by the Family Vision Statement) is the Family Council—a gathering of the family, overseen by elected family leaders, with a specific and formal agenda. The Family Council is:

> A regular and planned forum where all family members
> participate in activities and experiences designed to promote
> family unity, family values, and family traditions.

It may seem silly (and a little uncharacteristic of your family), but there are times when a touch of formality is necessary. No matter how loosey-goosey your family norm might be, there are occasions that demand a more methodical approach because there are matters of significant importance to be discussed and decided. The Family Council belongs in that category.

This doesn't mean every family member must dress up in a tuxedo and follow Robert's Rules of Order. It does mean that a bit of thought, a few basic rules, and some designated leadership is the most likely way your family will make progress toward its ultimate destination.

Leaders of the Family Council should be elected by the family, with one exception. Parents (who are exempt from serving themselves) should select the council leaders for an initial two-year period. As parents, you have a responsibility to groom and mentor the future leaders of your family. Don't expect these future leaders to do everything perfectly. They won't. Neither would you at their age (or even now!). Give them some grace, encourage them, and help them grow. But, whatever else you do, don't step in and do the job for them.

Formalizing—parents selecting leaders initially, family electing leaders eventually—provides a way to move family leadership out of the hands of the parents and into the hands of their heirs . . . to grow up the next generation of family leadership so that—in the leadership vacuum precipitated by the death of parents—others will be prepared and positioned to step into leadership roles.

The selected or elected positions will probably take the form of:

- Chairperson—charged with putting agenda items before the council, leading family discussions, calling for decisions, and making assignments.
- Secretary—charged with publishing a formal agenda, keeping minutes of the council meetings, and publishing those minutes in a timely way.
- Treasurer—charged with managing the council's funds, tracking accounts, and reporting developments to each council meeting.

Together, the elected leaders of the Family Council are responsible for the annual Family Retreats (setting the theme, determining the agenda, inviting participants, making arrangements, doing necessary follow-up) and calling other meetings of the Family Council as may be required by family business, finances, or concerns.

There are a few rules the family should observe when meeting together in Council:

- What the family says in the room stays in the room, unless everybody agrees otherwise.
- The welfare and harmony of the family is the most important consideration in any discussion about any topic. Winning a point at the cost of tension, disrespect, and disunity is always a loss in the Family Council.
- The published agenda should be respected in the family's discussions. Focus on the agenda. Don't let other, unplanned subjects dominate the family's time.

- Only one family member talks at a time, and everyone is given an opportunity (indeed, encouraged!) to have their say.
- Each person should keep an open mind about family business, debates, and decisions. Family discussions are about listening, understanding, and finding common ground. Stubbornness, defensiveness, and unyielding opinions have no place.
- Blame and personal attacks are counterproductive and not allowed.
- Everyone should feel free to talk about what they think and how they feel. This is a safe environment.

With just a few rules, a bit of leadership, and a little planning, the "business of being a family" can make giant strides forward. Members of the family can work cooperatively to reach goals that are important to the family as a whole. And the result will be not just the survival of your family's legacy but a vigorous and vital legacy to pass along to future generations.

Ongoing Retreats

At the conclusion of the initial Family Retreat, plans should be made for ongoing Family Retreats. If your family has embraced the notion of legacy, established a Family Council, and committed to regular meetings, the next retreat can be scheduled inside a year. (Typically, Family Retreats are held at least annually.)

These ongoing Family Retreats have three functions:

- Family fun
- Family education
- Family business

The "fun" part is important—just as important as the rest of the family business you conduct. Remember, you may have all kinds of people attending these retreats, including kids and grandkids, spouses, and (perhaps) extended family and mentors. Make sure there are plenty of activities lined up for "all shapes and sizes" to match the diversity of your family. Not every activity must be enjoyed *together*—you're not joined at the hip. But some of the planned activities should involve everyone. And all of them should encourage new groupings to form (no cliques!), opportunities for multigenerational mingling, and the making of memories that deepen family ties.

The "educational" component of the ongoing Family Retreats involves a continuation of the goals and objectives your family began to set at the initial retreat. It might include:

- An extended Guided Discovery experience for the whole family.
- Reflections and suggestions about the Family Vision Statement.
- Asking members of the family to tell their personal stories and (in the case of those who have married into the family) the stories of their family of origin.
- Activities that help members of the family become better listeners.
- Developing family philanthropy and cooperative generosity.
- Family leadership.
- Teamwork.
- Personal and family development.
- Faith, family, and finances (see the three chapters that conclude this book).

The opportunities to think as a family . . . about matters of importance to the family . . . in order to carry out the business of family . . . with the goal of furthering the family's legacy are many and varied. It doesn't matter how long your Family Retreats extend into the future—you will never run out of themes to pursue and ideas to discuss.

When it comes to conducting the "business" function of Family Retreats, the opportunities are more limited (perhaps) but also more focused.

- Discussing the inheritance heirs can expect to receive—and parental expectations about how that inheritance might bless the lives of family members.
- Understanding the "vehicles" to be used in conveying that inheritance: estate plans, wills, assessments, bequests, charitable trusts, etc.

- Discussing end-of-life issues: living wills, power of attorney, escrows, estate, executors, insurance policies, funeral arrangements, etc.
- Learning the ins and outs of family finances—including the family business(es), stock portfolio, partnerships, banking practices, investments, real estate, etc.
- Learning the family's philosophy of money: saving, investing, spending, tax management, charitable giving, etc.
- Becoming part of the family's philanthropic efforts: history, philosophy, institutional affiliations, etc.

Whatever themes are pursued during ongoing Family Retreats, and whatever discussions are projected for the future, the mix of fun, education, and family business will keep your family in touch with and engaged in the legacy you want to pass to the future. Equipping the family with a minimal structure for meetings, leadership, and discussion guidelines will ensure that the family's legacy is protected, practiced, and preserved for generations to come.

Conclusion

Don't forget that the heart of the Family Retreat involves the family's stories. The variety of the activities you experience at these retreats is good, but not good enough. The structures you put in place to foster productive retreats are necessary, but not sufficient. In the end, it all comes down to *stories*. Stories of grandparents, parents, and others who have struggled, built, succeeded, and just plain hung in there. Stories your children tell about growing up and learning life and finding meaning. Stories of your family's past and present . . . the projection of those stories into the future.

These stories should be given a place of honor in the life of your family. They are the parables that present timeless truths in palatable packages. They are poems scattered among the dusty recollections of family facts and dates. They are the barbs carved into the family's legacy to help that legacy stick in the hearts of your heirs. They are the portion of the Family Retreats your family will love best . . . the most powerful and profound part of the family time you will enjoy together.

Exercises

At the initial Family Retreat, you should initiate a "pre-inheritance" experience:

1. Set up a Family Bank—a fund established for the use of your children to encourage them to work cooperatively to accomplish a common goal.
2. The amount deposited in this account is irrelevant (although it should be enough to get the attention and encourage the efforts of your heirs).
3. Make clear that this bank is controlled by the heirs (not by you and your spouse).
4. Create guidelines to help your children understand the purpose of this bank and regulate their use of it.

   - They can't spend the capital/corpus.
   - They must invest the funds.
   - The goal is for the funds to earn more than passbook interest.
   - They can't ask Mom and Dad what to do with the funds.

This "pre-inheritance" experience will give parents an opportunity to see how well equipped and ready heirs are to work *together*, to work *effectively*, and to work *hard* with assets under their control—precisely the kind of challenge heirs will experience when they receive an inheritance at the time of your death.

Note

1. Matthew 13:35.

Section Three

POSSESSIONS AND PEOPLE OF FAITH

Section Three offers a primer in the attitudes people of faith cultivate toward possessions.

Obviously, disciples of Jesus should live differently from those who do not claim this allegiance. Our goals are different. Our lifestyles are distinct. We live by other values and mores. Our behaviors and attitudes are guided by a higher hand.

This is particularly true of our relationship with money. How we handle money, our attitudes toward it, and the place it assumes in our lives must be shaped by the teachings of our Lord. Jesus has a great deal to say to his followers about the link between faith and possessions. Faith changes our relationship with material things. It changes the value we place on money, the manner in which we use it, and the goals we pursue with it.

If there is no difference between Christians and non-Christians in our attitudes toward possessions, then we are not really listening to Jesus. He insists our lives must be measured by higher standards than the merely material. Possessions do not define our true worth. Others are free to spend their lives accumulating and amassing and acquiring. But Christians have more important matters to pursue with their time, energy, gifts . . . and money.

The three chapters in Section Three ask some basic questions about Christians and their money:

- What does God value (and where does money fit into that)?
- Why is my money God's business?
- When is "enough" enough?

These questions identify key attitudes that, as Christians, we need to develop as we relate to material things. As you read these chapters, you'll need to do some significant soul-searching. Do you agree with what you read here? Do you believe Christian commitment changes your relationship with money? Are you willing to put your money where your faith is?

If you haven't developed these attitudes toward possessions (or if you are unwilling to do so), there is little chance you will be able to teach these attitudes to your heirs. But these attitudes are foundational for preparing your heirs to handle their inheritance in godly ways.

CHAPTER ELEVEN

GOD'S ECONOMY

What God Values

She was down to her last dime—literally. Her clothes hung in rags from her thin frame. She'd been sleeping rough for weeks now, in doorways and town squares. Her hair hung lank and lifeless from a face lined with fatigue. She smelled faintly of ripe cheese.

A dime would buy her a heel of bread. Perhaps a few beans to go with it. It might be enough to keep body and soul together while she swallowed her dignity and held out her hand for some stranger's alms. Another dime for another day. Another dime to prolong the ache in her stomach and the ache in her heart.

In the end, though, with husband dead and no children to shelter her from the dark of her declining days, dimes tossed from pity would not be enough. In the end, she knew, there would be a quiet corner of some wood, a secluded nook in a field, where she would lay herself down and give herself to God.

But not today.

She looked up to the towering heights of the Temple Mount and the majestic walls that were its crown. In the light of dying day, the stone of the temple shone with a golden glow, as if the light of God were pulsing from within and beckoning her into his presence. She lurched forward on unsteady feet, heeding the call.

By the time she made the climb and pushed herself through Solomon's Portico, through the crowds milling about the Court of the Gentiles, and into the Court of Women, she was done. Her head swam and her knees buckled. She joined a queue just for the support it provided—a body in front and a body behind. It took a few moments for her head to clear enough to realize she was in the offering line formed before the temple treasury.

The laugh, when it found her, shook her and wrenched her and would not let her go. The people around her stared and then looked away. She did not care. It had been long years since she'd laughed.

But when the laugh left her, she did not leave the line. There was something fitting, she realized, about standing among the rich with her thin dime and her thin prospects to make an offering to God. Her dime wouldn't matter to the Temple—*that* she knew. But perhaps it would matter to God, this dime that might sustain her for one more day given to the God who had sustained her all her days.

Can a dime be a prayer? she wondered. Perhaps not a plea for a better tomorrow. A dime was a small coin for such a large hope. But a dime—a last dime—could say "Thank you" well enough. For the better days of years gone by. For blessings enjoyed and lost.

When the line led her to the offering box, she dropped in her dime without hesitation or regret and moved away to greet what remained of her life. She left with no new hopes. She heard no promises whispered as the dime dropped. But her heart, even her legs, felt lighter just the same.

Across the way, an arm pointed toward her. A man leaned in close to the faces fixed on him. He spoke a few words. "More. More than all the others." They nodded, bewildered. He turned from them to watch the widow make her lonely way across the temple courts to an uncertain future. His eyes shone like the walls of the temple, as if the light of God was pulsing within him, beckoning her to himself.[1]

The "Money" Subject

Among the most difficult issues facing American Christians is the relationship we have (or are supposed to have) with possessions. We know that wearing the name "Christian" should change the way we think about, use, and value things. And we know that Jesus had a great deal to say on the matter. But it's a relationship we have trouble talking about. Much of what Jesus said about possessions is not easy to hear. Some of what he said is downright disturbing.

At the heart of Jesus' teachings about possessions, however, are a few simple lessons we must take to heart if we call ourselves Christians and believe that Jesus—even in this matter—is Lord.

The story of the Widow's Mite (Mark 12:41–44) points us to a fundamental truth. To get at it, a little honesty is required.

The character we most resemble in this parable is *not* the widow. Oh, we like to cast ourselves in her role as we read the story: giving our all . . . trusting God that much . . . commended by Jesus. But the truth is, most of us have never been that poor, that destitute. We've never been down to our last dime.

If we resemble anyone in this story, it's the other people standing in line with the widow. We are the rich ones. (Even the poorest of us is rich by any historical or worldwide measure.) We come to the temple with our cash and our checks. When we give, we give out of our wealth . . . we give the income that is disposable . . . we give the money we don't absolutely need for other priorities.

I point this out not to chastise or shame us. I'm glad we're standing in line! I'm thankful that we think about God when check-writing time comes. But to learn the lesson of this story, we must recognize that it is not really about the different kinds of people lining up to give—rich or poor, stingy or generous. The point of the story is not that we all should become penniless widows . . . that only those who have nothing can offer God something of value.

What Jesus teaches in this story is actually about God. God is present as a witness to these proceedings. He sees what gifts are brought. But he doesn't measure these gifts as we often do: by their size or the percentage of income they represent. He assesses other values, other currencies, as he measures the kind and worth of the gifts we offer.

A Dollar Bill

Where your treasure is, there your heart will be also. (Matt. 6:21)

Reach into your wallet and pull out a dollar bill.

Buck . . . Greenback . . . Clam . . . Simoleon . . . Washington . . . Ace. We know the dollar bill by many names.

We've all seen dollars stretch and shrink and run short. You can bet your bottom one and ask your top one. Some people feel (or look) like a million of them. Certain questions are worth sixty-four thousand of them.

We refer to the dollar (and its higher denomination cousins) as "paper money." But, in fact, the dollar bill is made of fabric (75 percent cotton, 25 percent linen, with negligible traces of red and blue synthetic fibers thrown in). It can be folded, spindled, and mutilated (even washed!) and still do its job.

It costs about four cents to produce a dollar bill. Our government prints over sixteen million of them every day!

And since 1957, the phrase "In God We Trust" has been printed on every US one-dollar bill.

That's ironic, don't you think? On the one thing we're tempted to trust more than God, there is a printed reminder of where our trust is best placed. On the chief competitor for our affection and confidence and reliance and dependency, there is a printed prompt to rely on God above all else. It's shocking . . . jarring . . . and a bit confrontive, when you actually stop to think about it.

Is the dollar bill right? *Should* we trust in God? *Do* we trust in God? Most people, frankly, do not. At least, not more than in George Washington and his compadres: Lincoln, Hamilton, Jackson, Grant, and Franklin. Trust in the Almighty Dollar is far more common than trust in Almighty God.

But what about people of faith? What about those who claim trust in God as the defining attribute of their lives? Do *we* trust in God? Do *we* trust in him more than we trust in money?

That's a hard question to answer. In today's money-obsessed, consumer-oriented, wealth-celebrating, dollar-dependent culture, it's easy for Christians to *say* they trust in God first and foremost.

But we're still uncomfortably fond of those green and black swatches of fabric graced with the face of our first president.

Money from God's Perspective

> *What is highly valued among men is detestable in God's sight.*
> *(Luke 16:15)*

God doesn't think like we do. His values are different. What is important to him isn't always important to us. What *we* prize, *he* often regards with a shrug and a yawn.

Take money as an example.

Money is important to us (be honest!). Making it, accumulating it, accruing a surfeit of it accounts for large portions of our energy, time, and attention. When you add up all the hours we spend earning a dollar, all the effort we expend chasing it, all the single-minded focus we devote in pursuit of it, you'll find we trade off significant portions of our lives to achieve the standard of living to which we long to become accustomed!

For most of us—in truth—it isn't the money itself that holds the attraction. We wouldn't think of jumping into a pile of coins to wallow and revel in their cold comfort (like Scrooge McDuck of cartoon fame).

But we do appreciate what money *buys*: ease, opportunity, freedom, security, provision, control, even power. Money makes it possible for us to establish a certain standard of living, to provide housing and transportation, to purchase iPads and Internet access, to save for retirement, and to afford the occasional Starbucks. It lets us put our kids through college and feed and clothe our families. Those who have money enjoy all manner of prospects and privileges. Most of us would rather struggle with the dangers of too much money than with the deprivations of too little.

So, while it is not money *per se* that we love, we do dearly love the things money permits us.

And we love how money makes us *feel*. (Warning, we're treading on dangerous territory here!) With money, we can feel comfortable and full. With money, we can provide for a basic sense of safety and security. With money, we can achieve the euphoric conviction that we are independent, empowered, admired, benevolent, blessed, special, and confident. Maybe money can buy happiness after all!

Not so fast . . .

Have I mentioned that God's values are different? That, ultimately, is the point of the story of the Widow's Mite. Jesus looked at the people standing in line to donate to the temple treasury. And without blush or hesitation, he told his disciples that the person who gave the gift most valued by God was the person who made the smallest financial donation. God uses a different yardstick when he thinks about what is valuable, what is important, what matters most. In God's economy, the number of zeros that appear on the "amount" line of the check isn't the point.

God's system of values and priorities, the purposes he is pursuing in our world, the "treasures" he wants to distribute to us are not primarily *financial*. While money has a place in God's economy, it is not the *primary* place that money occupies in more worldly economies.

God wants us to be "rich." He has "treasure" and "fine pearls" in store for us. He promises a "throne" and a "crown" and a fabulous "inheritance" to us. But God defines spiritual wealth in spiritual ways. The "currencies" that are most important to God have little to do with material tender.

God's Economy

While we tend to measure value by dollars and cents, God thinks in different terms.

God is more concerned with *character* currencies than with financial ones. Are you humble? Do you have integrity? Have you learned the secret of being content? These qualities of character are more treasured by God than the size of your bank account. A good person who owns nothing is far richer in God's economy than a corrupt person who enjoys every comfort and privilege.

God appreciates *faith* currencies. Do you put God first? Do you trust him in everything? Are you obedient to his commands? Is worship and praise something you love? Do you avoid worry? These attributes of faith are, in God's estimation, a truer indicator of wealth than investment portfolios and net worth. The one who believes is infinitely richer in God's economy than the one who balks and resists—no matter the size of their estate.

God sees treasure in certain *relational* currencies. Are you a person who treats people right? Do you love your neighbor as yourself? Are you quick to show compassion? Will you forgive those who sin against you? These relational habits are of greater value to God than anything that can be measured financially. Those who care about others—whether rich or poor—have wealth that those who care only for themselves can never possess.

Seen from this spiritual perspective, money has no eternal value in and of itself. It is a resource, a tool, an instrument for higher purposes. Like much that is rooted in the physical realm—health, time, intelligence, energy— God views money as a *means* by which we pursue matters that ultimately matter. Used in godly ways—in acts of mercy, for ministry, in support of kingdom priorities—money can be a great blessing. But used in less-than-godly ways—for the merely physical, for "building bigger barns," for pursuing priorities that focus on ourselves rather than the kingdom—money can become a curse.

God doesn't need money to accomplish his purposes. In particular, God doesn't require that *we* have money or possessions or wealth to accomplish his purposes in *us*. Money cannot buy the things that God values most: character, faith, healthy relationships. And money can never make us feel what God alone can provide. When we use money to purchase qualities of life that only God delivers, we demonstrate a trust in money that has no place in the lives of believers. Our security, meaning, provision, confidence, empowerment, freedom, and worth are meant to be found in *him*, not in *it*.

What money *can* do is leave a paper trail about the condition of our hearts. The debits in our checkbooks and on our credit card statements represent a sure indicator of what we value and what we believe to be important. They tell God (and others) where our hearts are, where our priorities lie, what we truly love. How we use money demonstrates what we view as valuable and whether we see life from the perspective of the world or the perspective of the eternal.

Money follows the heart. And it is our *hearts*, above all else, God prizes.

Jesus and Money

Jesus told the story of this poor widow because he wanted his disciples (and us) to discover something about God. Jesus simply wants us to understand that God values things differently than we do. Money is not his principal measure of what is valuable. To him, treasures are things we might not consider all that precious: trust . . . kindness . . . contentment . . . mercy . . . prayer . . . gratitude.

In the end, only what we give God makes us rich. Not what we save and accumulate. Not how many barns we build or how many things we own. The widow had more to offer than all the others because she gave everything to God. She held nothing back. And Jesus applauded her for that, recognizing how precious (and rare) such an attitude was.

And only when we give God what *he* values can we consider ourselves wealthy. Give God your money, by all means. But recognize that sizeable financial gifts in the absence of humility and penitence are baubles and trinkets in God's eyes. True wealth, from God's perspective, is measured by the size of the heart rather than the size of the donation.

The woman we meet in this story gave God her trusting heart and was blessed for doing so. The Good Samaritan offered the gift of compassion and has become more famous than many kings and billionaires. The woman who washed Jesus' feet with costly perfume was pouring out her gratitude—a costly gift indeed. The tax collector who appeared at the temple to beat his breast and beg God's mercy gave God the gift of his penitence—and was sent home with the treasure of God's forgiveness. Strange gifts when viewed from the economy of this world but, when seen from God's economic perspective, true treasure . . . great riches . . . enormous wealth.

While we are tempted to define ourselves by money, to measure our worth by our portfolios, Jesus insists that life—real life—has to be about *more*. "Life is not measured by how much you own" (Luke 12:15 NLT). There are other qualities that define us in God's sight, other "currencies" that give us value.

When we learn what really matters to God, when we make the attributes God appreciates a priority in our lives, when we set our hearts on things eternal, we "store up treasures in heaven" . . . true riches . . . greater and more reliable wealth than anything that can be measured by a bank account (Matt. 6:19–20).

Where Is Your Treasure?

"In God We Trust" proclaim our dollar bills. Is it true? Is it true of you?

Trusting in God means valuing what he values. Trusting in God means trafficking in the currencies that have spiritual worth. Trusting in God means choosing between your Father and your wallet as the primary source of your identity and merit.

As we think about passing on a legacy to those who come after us, the first thing we must recognize is that *our hearts are our heirs' most basic inheritance.* Before they receive our bequests, they learn our values. Before the will is read, they read our perspectives and priorities and the principles by which we live.

What do you care about? Where do you invest the best of yourself? What "master" do you serve?

Your children know. They see you living out your priorities every day. They can sense where your heart is, what you really value, what constitutes "first things" for you.

Legacy begins with the heart. When your heart belongs to the kingdom, possessions take their proper place as means to eternal ends. And your heirs have a chance to learn the proper weight of the material.

When, instead, your heart belongs to your possessions, don't be surprised when your children define "treasure" as you do and place their hearts where you have.

Exercises

1. List three ministries or organizations where you see God at work and which you believe to be worthy of financial support.

2. Which do you trust more: God or money? What evidence can you provide? Is this evidence obvious to your heirs?

3. Are you addicted to (over-involved in) activities or hobbies that are consuming valuable time and resources that could be put to better use for kingdom purposes? What are they?

4. Are your stewardship responsibilities evident to your heirs through your actions and the way you use money? Can your heirs see that *generosity* is important to you? How?

5. This chapter discusses other currencies (nonfinancial currencies) that God highly values. How would you rate yourself in *character* currencies? Are you, for instance, demonstrating the fruit of the Spirit—Galatians 5:22–23?

6. How would you rate yourself in *faith* currencies? Do you, for instance, tend to walk by faith or by sight—2 Corinthians 5:7?

7. How would you rate yourself in *relationship* currencies? Like loving your neighbor, living by the Golden Rule, showing mercy.

Note
____

1. Mark 12:41–44.

CHAPTER TWELVE

MY MONEY IS GOD'S BUSINESS

The Call to Stewardship

He wasn't a bad man, as men go.

There were no horrid and heinous sins of which he was guilty . . . no taboo indulgences he furtively permitted himself . . . no secret life he was obliged to hide from the neighbors.

To the contrary. Everything we know about this man testifies to competence and diligence and nose-to-the-grindstone industry. Up before dawn. Labor all day. Accounts each evening. The parable Jesus told about this man is a testimony to well-managed lands, frugal ways, and good agrarian practices. Crops were in the ground at their proper time in spring. Sprouts were weeded and watered through summer. Come fall, the harvest was carefully, capably gathered.

One year, all this competence and diligence and industry paid off. The sun smiled on his fields. The rain fell regularly and generously. The harvest proved bountiful.

The farmer realized he had so much grain, he didn't know what to do!

The ground of a certain rich man yielded an abundant harvest. He thought to himself, "What shall I do? I have no place to store my crops."

Then he said, "This is what I'll do. I will tear down my barns and build bigger ones, and there I will store my surplus grain. And I'll say to myself, 'You have plenty of grain laid up for many years. Take life easy; eat, drink and be merry.'"

But God said to him, "You fool! This very night your life will be demanded from you. Then who will get what you have prepared for yourself?"

This is how it will be with whoever stores up things for themselves but is not rich toward God. (Luke 12:16–21)

Putting Distance between the Rich Man and Us

We readers of this parable have slandered the rich man mercilessly. We've caricatured him as a greedy and rapacious violator of the land, extorting profits from the sweaty brows and bloody backs of his servants, a robber-baron figure for whom enough is never enough. In our minds, he twirls his mustache as he cackles over profit margins and despoils helpless maidens in his spare time.

We've read this story and added salacious details, not because the details are plainly there in the story for any discerning reader to find (they are not!) but to distance this man—to distinguish him—from ourselves. He sounds too normal. His question ("What shall I do?") and especially his answer ("Build bigger barns!") seem perfectly reasonable to us. There must be more to the story that explains why God would call this man a fool. I bet he beat his dog!

As materially blessed people ourselves, as barn-builders and crop-accumulators of the first rank, as people who dream of retiring to Florida and riding gently into the night on a golf cart, we identify with this poor rich farmer. He sounds like us.

According to the story, this fellow earned his money honestly. He sowed a crop and reaped a harvest. His hard work resulted in an "abundant profit."

This story does not hint at worker exploitation or environmental rapine or tax evasion or ill-gotten booty. He made an honest profit and then used that profit to build barns, not indulge in wine, women, and song (well, maybe a little wine). All he wanted was to relax a little in the future . . . to escape the daily grind of scrabbling for every advantage and comfort.

The question he asks—What shall I do with all my crops?—is answered in a very businesslike and prudent way: "I'll save. I'll protect the investment I've made by structuring for continued profitability. I'll build bigger barns to hold more crops. I'll set something aside in the present for the future . . . for my retirement." What's wrong with that?

The Parable of the Rich Fool is difficult for us to read precisely because this man is a lot like us! Frankly, his "sin" doesn't seem all that terrible. Thinking ahead, investing, and planning for the future are sound fiscal practices. He answers the question about what to do with his abundance exactly as you and I would . . . *as we have*!

So why does God consider him a fool? Surely there's some despicable, vile secret hiding just beneath the surface of this man's life . . . and behind the thin veneer of the story.

A Fool?

Such a strong word—*fool*. Didn't Jesus warn us against using dismissive terms like this? Wasn't this a slur Jesus reserved for people who had the hardest hearts and demonstrated the greatest opposition to his ministry? Why would he use this term about this man in this parable? It raises some serious questions.

Does God have a problem with rich people?

We know he loves penniless beggars, the helpless, and the deprived. There is a special place in his heart for widows and orphans—people on the margins. But what about those who have more than a couple of mites to rub together? Does God care about them? Of course he does. We know that God loved David—the fabulously wealthy king. And Job—"the richest person in the East." And Abraham—a man "very wealthy in livestock and in silver and gold." And Zacchaeus—the affluent tax collector.

Does God have a problem with profits?

Some people read this parable as an anticapitalistic morality play. "God doesn't mind us eking out a meager living," such readers might say, "living hand-to-mouth, getting by with subsistent standards of living. But he has a problem when our profits go up, when margins widen, when we harvest too abundantly." This reading turns the parable into an indictment on making money.

Really? Surely that casts God as a miserly curmudgeon who takes more pleasure in our privation than our prospering. And, if you think about it, this "profit" was God's doing anyway! He sent the rain and sun that produced this abundant harvest. It was his generous outpouring that caused the rich man's profit problem in the first place!

Does God have a problem with planning for the future . . . with saving and investing?

There are too many other stories and teachings in Scripture (leading to the opposite conclusion) for us to believe that.

God didn't call this farmer a fool because he was wealthy or because he enjoyed an abundant harvest or because he chose to invest for the future.

A Problem with Pronouns

God had a problem with this man because this man had a problem with *pronouns*.

> He thought to himself, "What shall I do? I have no place to store my crops."
>
> Then he said, "This is what I'll do. I will tear down my barns and build bigger ones, and there I will store my surplus grain. And I'll say to myself, 'You have plenty of grain laid up for many years. Take life easy; eat, drink and be merry.'"

You don't have to listen very closely to this internal dialogue to hear how the rich man *thought*. He was having a conversation with himself, about himself and his resources, without reference to anyone else but himself. God was not included in the discussion. No higher values informed the man's deliberations than his own comfort and his personal future.

The crops were *his*. The barns were *his*. The grain was *his*. The decision about what to do with it all was *his*. *His* priorities and interests and perspectives were the only ones that mattered when it came to his possessions. *His* plans and hopes were the driving factors about how those possessions were used. This man believed that his money was his business, that he could dispose of his profits as he pleased, that he was the one to decide what to do with this "abundant harvest."

Notice how God picked up on these pesky pronouns: "But God said to him, '*You* fool! This very night *your* life will be demanded from *you*. Then who will get what *you* have prepared for *yourself*?'"

The pronouns tell us a great deal about the rich man's attitudes. This stuff was his. What he did with it was his business. God did not enter the picture. God certainly had no right to meddle in the man's personal and financial decisions.

And that is why God calls this man a fool.

So shortsighted was this poor rich man, so narrow in his perspectives, that he failed to recognize it was God who created the land on which he planted his crops, God who set the seasons, God who put into seed the miracle of life. It was God who placed the sun in the sky and brought clouds ripe with rain. It was God who put breath in this man's lungs and permitted him the energy and health to farm and provided him with time and resources. It was God who gave the man his very life.

By ignoring this God-sized context, the rich farmer demonstrated that he was "not rich toward God." By leaving God out of the conversation, he showed the kind of "fool" he truly was.

Because only a fool forgets that it is God who gives . . . and God who takes away.

A Foolish Perspective on Money

This foolish, self-absorbed, acquisitive rich man would fit right into modern American culture. He would be welcomed into our neighborhoods and clubs. He could move in next door, and we wouldn't think anything was odd. He could even attend our church, and not a single spiritual alarm would sound.

This rich man isn't a breed apart. He isn't some strange and rare beast stalking our unsuspecting streets. This is a man we recognize. This is a man we know. He is us.

Modern culture does a great job of raising up people just like this rich man. It does so by perpetuating a few myths about wealth.

It tells us first that wealth grows out of hard work and competence and best business practices and self-reliance. Wealth comes from long hours and calloused hands and nose-to-the-grindstone effort. Wealth is the fruit that grows from the seeds of creativity, business acumen, market prescience, and personal skill.

Wealth—in a word—is rooted in the soil of "me."

Our culture also tells us that—when we work so hard to earn something—we have the right to regard the fruits of our labor as *ours*. We *own* what we work for. It belongs to us. It is ours to dispose of as we please. These are *my* crops, *my* barns, *my* surplus grain.

Wealth that grows out of "me"—wealth that I create—is mine.

And, finally, our culture whispers that the point of all that earning and owning is to care for our needs and ensure a more comfortable future for ourselves. The *purpose* of accumulating an abundance is to provide for our personal security, comfort, and enjoyment.

Wealth created by *me and belonging* to *me is* for *me.*

Our culture teaches us to use the rich fool's pronouns: me, my, mine. Our ready use of those pronouns says as much about us as it did about him. It indicates we think more like this man than we might care to admit.

Don't imagine that going to church inoculates us against this kind of thinking. Just the opposite. Church has become the culture's ally in raising up rich fools. It has embraced and inculcated the fool's perspective on wealth. At the extreme, pulpits are pounded regularly on behalf of a "health and wealth" gospel—a theological Ponzi scheme that equates prosperity with spirituality and baptizes wealth as the disciple's right and privilege. But even in the mainstream, pulpits too often proclaim that wealth is from us, belongs to us, and is for us. "Tithe!" goes the common message. "Give a little of your abundance to God. But keep the rest and do with it what you want."

Churches are eagerly baptizing rich foolery as normal Christian behavior.

A Wise Perspective on Money

There is another way to think about wealth. We aren't *required* to reason like rich fools when it comes to possessions. There is a Christ-informed perspective, a faith-shaped attitude, that offers a distinctly different view of our relationship with money.

It is an alternative perspective that uses alternative pronouns—*thee* instead of *me*. It is an alternative perspective that imagines an alternative conversation—including God rather than "thinking to ourselves." It is an alternative perspective that poses an alternative relationship with wealth—not *owners* but *stewards*.

This alternative perspective is rooted in the notion of God as Creator. He made the world and all that is in it. He created time—all of our years, months, and days . . . every second. He formed the very "stuff" which makes work and wealth possible: energy, creativity, skill, resources, relationships, persistence, intelligence.

As Creator, everything belongs to God. All that exists is his. From a theological perspective, there is no "mine" or "ours"—there is only "his." Every resource and element and commodity. Every quality and attribute and trait and ability. Every valuable and bauble, every trinket and trifle and treasure. Every pod and seed. Every crop. Every barn. Every acre of fertile soil. Every drop of moisture that falls from the sky. Every sunbeam. Every season.

The "wise perspective" understands that wealth grows out of the soil of "him."

As a sign of his love and respect, God graciously shares his resources with us. He gives good gifts to his children: daily bread and clothes to cover and a roof overhead. He is a generous God who wants to take care of us. He knows our needs. He provides for us in every way—including the material.

The "wise perspective" understands that God shares his wealth with his children.

That word "shared" is important, however. Sharing does not imply transfer of ownership. Just because God graciously shares his resources with us does not mean those resources become ours. We can manage God's resources, take care of them, watch over them, prove trustworthy with them. We can even benefit from them, be sustained by them. But we do not *own* those resources . . . they do not become our property, to dispose of as we please, without regard to anyone or anything else. Everything God shares with us remains his.

The "wise perspective" understands that we are stewards of God's resources, not possessors of them . . . that his wealth, even when shared with us, remains "his."

Which leads, finally, to the question: What is wealth *for*?

God's Barns

The Rich Fool focused so exclusively on his own barns that he forgot God has barns of his own to build. He has his own goals to think about. He is pursuing his own plans and purposes.

God's barns are bigger than ours . . . *other* than ours. There is more at stake in the future God contemplates. His kingdom business cannot be limited to one field or one farmer or one set of retirement goals.

Here's the wrinkle. God is perfectly capable of growing his own crops, tending to his own fields, gathering in his own harvest, building his own barns. But that's not how he works. Instead, God is committed to working through us, partnering with us, to accomplish his kingdom business.

He shares his resources with us and then invites us to share his mission with him.

From God's perspective, there are lives to touch, hearts to shape, mercy to show, scars to heal. There are souls to win, minds to engage, courage to inspire, hope to instill. There's a world to turn upside down, forces of evil to rout, people to grow up into the fullness of Christ. Opportunities abound for generosity and selfless service and kingdom influence.

The question is: Will we use God's resources to pursue God's goals? Will we understand our role as God's middlemen, funneling his resources toward his purposes as faithfully as possible? Or will we focus only on the barns of our personal desire?

We should expect God to take care of us as we serve him as stewards. He fully anticipates that some of the resources he shares with us will be used for our own sustenance and purposes. God has never been greedy, intending to wring a rich spiritual harvest from the sweaty brows and bloody backs of those who serve him.

But God also expects us to recognize that we did not generate these material resources ourselves; *he* created them. He wants us to acknowledge that whatever we "possess" is a blessing from him, a sharing in *his* resources. He asks us to admit that the resources remain his rather than ours, that we are the stewards and managers of those resources, not the owners. And he urges us to accept the notion that—ultimately—God's resources are meant to be used for God's purposes.

It is not difficult, then, to imagine God's shock when he discovers that the resources he has entrusted to us are being highjacked in their entirety for our personal plans and purposes! He overhears us pondering what to do with our abundance and deciding, without reference to him, to build the barns that suit us best. He hears the pronouns we use—me, my, mine—and the plans we make—plenty, for many years, take it easy—and shakes his head sadly.

"You're storing up for yourselves. But you are not rich toward me! How foolish!"

Imagine

What if *every* believer understood (deeply and sincerely) that all good things come from God?

What if *every* believer recognized (absolutely and gratefully) that all the things we have and enjoy belong to God, but they are shared with us as a sign of his love and care?

What if *every* believer accepted (enthusiastically) the idea that we act as stewards of God's resources and have a responsibility to do his business with his assets?

What if *every* believer valued (first and foremost) God's barns over our own?

What if *every* believer were a steward? What would that look like? What difference could that make? Here are a few ideas:

1. Stewards would tithe to their church.
2. Stewards would eagerly seek out worthy ministries and charities to support with their time, energy, and money—or (rather) with the time, energy, and money God has entrusted to them.

3. Stewards would ooze generosity every day—with people who "accidentally" cross their paths . . . with neighbors . . . with people at work and play. The characteristic response of a *steward* to people in need would be, "How can I help?" rather than "Leave me alone."

4. Stewards would see and seize the opportunity to "build God's barns" at the time of their death. They would devote some portion of their possessions (10 percent? . . . the proceeds of a life-insurance policy? . . . some portion of an IRA?) to a worthy work that helps expand God's kingdom. A ministry. A mission effort. An institution pursuing godly ends. A church or Christian school.

5. And stewards would recognize the opportunity (at their passing) to encourage generosity in their heirs. To model generosity, certainly. But also to *advocate* generosity—explicitly and boldly—as one of the great joys and solemn responsibilities of being richly blessed.

Imagine a world in which all believers were stewards of God's assets. Every church would be overfunded, forcing the question, "How can we do more good?" Every ministry would have the chance to reach higher and further. Every Christian school would get to expand its offerings and extend its influence. Every mission effort could fund missionaries and services and testimony.

Imagine a world where we built God's barns first . . . where all believers were rich toward God rather than storing up things for themselves.

Think of what God's people could accomplish! Think of what God could do if his resources were freed up to support his true business! Think of the difference it would make to our world!

In a world where believers were devoted to building God's barns, more of us might hear—when it comes time to give our lives back to God—"Well done, good and faithful Steward. You have been faithful with a few things; I will put you in charge of many things. Come and share your master's happiness!"

Exercises

1. Are you actively contributing to your local church? Are you contributing generously? Are you contributing sacrificially?

2. Are you presently supporting ministries or good works above and beyond your donations to your church?

3. Do you believe those ministries or good works will miss your donations and support when you die? What impact might the absence of your support have on these worthy efforts?

4. Have you considered a bequest in your will to "endow" your present support for the future? For example, if you are giving $1000 annually to XYZ kingdom work, a bequest of $25,000 in your will ensures that your support of that work can continue after you're gone, in perpetuity. ($25,000 x 4 percent annual interest = $1000 of interest income per year.)

Note

1. Mark 12:41–44.

CHAPTER THIRTEEN

WHEN IS "ENOUGH" ENOUGH?

Choosing a Standard of Living

"It's the weeds you have to watch out for," he told the boy. The crowd around him, as usual, was large. But today he saw only the young man—clear-eyed, shock of black hair falling over his forehead, his whole life before him. "The weeds will get you if you're not careful."

What weeds? the boy wanted to ask. *There are no weeds around here—just sand and scrub. What are you talking about?*

Jesus tried harder. "I'm a farmer. You are the soil. And the words I speak are God's seeds." He smiled. "But there are always weeds, you know . . . trying to choke out the better things in your heart."

The boy looked around at his friends, brow furrowed, shoulders hunched with incomprehension. He was missing something. He shifted weight from one foot to another, clawing nervously at his scalp and clothing.

Jesus kept on, relentless. "The seed won't stand a chance in many people. It will be snatched away before they even know it's there." He saw the concentration written in wrinkles on the boy's face. The boy wanted to understand. He was trying to understand.

"Some people hear my words. But tomorrow's sufferings, tomorrow's disappointments, will parch them and scorch them and burn away any hope of a crop. That could happen to you." He nodded at his young friend, his voice heavy with regret. The boy lowered his eyes to stare at his sandals.

"I can't keep Satan from stealing your faith. I cannot protect you from tomorrow's pain. But I can warn you about the weeds." He spoke softly now, as if the warning were for the boy alone. "As you get older, you'll worry about food and clothes. You'll focus on how much you have and how much you want. You'll let a craving for money, and for the things money can buy, grow inside you. And, if you are not careful, if you do not weed your heart, those worries will overwhelm what I'm telling you today."

He almost reached out for the boy, a hand to his shoulder to strengthen his words. "Don't make that mistake, son. Don't let money—worrying about it, making it, storing it away for the future—crowd out God's best treasure for you. Watch out for the weeds."[1]

How Much Is Enough?

Someone put that question to John D. Rockefeller once upon a time. He was a wealthy man, a millionaire many times over. He was powerful *because* he was wealthy . . . influential *because* he controlled so much money. He (quite literally) had more money than he could ever spend in a lifetime.

So, someone wondered, how much money was "enough" for a man like Rockefeller? How much would it take to satisfy him, to persuade him to cease his striving and struggling? What would it take for him to push back from the table of life and say, "I am content"?

Rockefeller's answer is enlightening. It says a lot about his state of mind regarding material things. It tells us much about his attitude toward money.

"Just a little more."

Just a little more than he had . . . just a little more than he'd acquire tomorrow . . . just a little more than he needed . . . just a little more than he could ever use . . . just a little more than others . . . just a little more than anyone.

You and I are no Rockefeller. But the question of "enough" is a valid question for us to consider. The answer we give may be just as enlightening.

How much is enough for you? What would it take for you to say, "What I have is sufficient"?

Something defines "enough" for each of us. Some standard, some bench-mark, some level of acquisition. You may not be able to put "enough" into words just now, to define it and label it and write a figure on paper. The answer, for you, may be a vague "more than I had growing up," or "more than I have now," or "enough so I don't depend on a paycheck," or "enough so people will respect me."

Something defines "enough" for you. Do you know what it is?

Enough = What I Want

Some people define "enough" as having everything they want. Not possessing *everything*, mind you . . . not all the money in the world or every gadget or house in the country or fancy car. Just everything they *desire*. Everything they crave and yearn for. The ability to satisfy the clamoring of their latest fixation.

So many people (especially so many Americans) have honed their con-sumer reflexes to razor sharpness. "I came, I saw, I whipped out my credit card" (*Veni, Vidi, Visa*). Whether their income matches their desires isn't a consideration. (Why should I limit myself to what I can actually afford?) Whether they can pay tomorrow for the object they purchased today isn't a consideration. (I'll let tomorrow worry about itself!) And God certainly isn't a consideration. Not his will or his kingdom or his priorities.

All that matters is that we *want* . . . the fact of our desire . . . the hunger to have . . . the power of possession. The id rises within us, mindless and slavering. We want what we want when we want it.

Focus on
what I want

Purchase

Momentary thrill

Consequences follow
(debt, obligation, burden)

Feelings of regret, remorse,
emptiness, guilt

Need to assuage
negative feelings

And a destructive cycle is set off by the primacy of our cravings:
This cycle describes a treadmill of unrestrained consumerism. Desire leads to possession which leads to an artificial and ephemeral joy. We feel powerful and happy and satisfied and complete. We congratulate ourselves on being successful. We revel in living the dream.

But tomorrow always comes. And with it come the bills and the payments and the indebtedness and the constrained options and the sense of burden. That, also, is a necessary (if unwelcome) part of this cycle: buyer's remorse . . . the crush of indebtedness. The ache returns and is intensified. We feel the emptiness, the oppression, the lack of contentment, the yammering need for something that satisfies.

And, so, off we go again—credit cards in hand—seeking to fill the emptiness with more stuff, hoping to purchase meaning at the cost of an Apple product, trying to ease the ache with another round of glutting our consumer appetites. The cycle recycles.

The Bible calls this tragic cycle *greed*: putting a desire for things ahead of good sense, personal peace, tomorrow's security, and God's kingdom.

Enough = What Others Have

Others of us, however, do not allow raw appetite to control our behavior. We recognize the immaturity of living by the Almighty Want. We don't run around the mall with twenty-five credit cards, buying anything that strikes our fickle fancy. We recognize there must be some limits to our desires.

And the limit we often choose is the standard of living set by our friends and peers and neighbors. "Enough" is what they have.

We don't want the sun and moon . . . we just want what others possess. We don't expect to enjoy every object of our desire . . . we just expect to have what our peers enjoy. Possession is not the point . . . *equity* is what we're after. If *they* have something, we should have it, too. If they enjoy certain perks and privileges, it is only right that we—as their equals—should enjoy the same.

And so we look around to find a group of people to serve as "comparables." People about our age and stage of life. People who share our education and earning potential. People in similar careers who should have equal earning potential. The idea is to find someone to whom we can hitch our standard of "enough."

We're not completely unrealistic in this. We don't measure ourselves by the Rockefellers among us . . . or the Trumps . . . or the Bill and Melinda Gateses of this world. We don't expect to live the lifestyle of the rich and famous.

But neither are we too modest. We wouldn't consider South American peasants or African villagers to be "comparables" for us. No outdoor latrines and limited caloric intake for us!

We find people who are like us and then spend our lives trying to live just like them. Never mind that these "comparables" are similar only in the most surface and superficial ways. Never mind that their values are significantly different from ours. Never mind that they have made no commitments to something higher, greater, or nobler in their lives. Never mind that they have chosen a standard of living that is unsatisfying and—ultimately—unsustainable.

If they drive a new Toyota, we'll buy a new Accord. If they have a sixty-inch plasma, we'll shop for a sixty-five-inch LED with an Internet connection. If they vacation in Hawaii . . . if they put in a home VAC system . . . if they eat at expensive restaurants . . . if they join certain clubs . . . if they take up particular hobbies. . . .

Keeping up with the Joneses becomes our defining mission in life. The resulting cycle is predictable, inevitable, and lamentable:

Focus on what others possess

Develop a sense of entitlement to those same possessions

Spend/borrow to a level that permits equity

Expect acceptance, approval, respect, praise of peers

Consequences follow (debt, obligation, burden) while expected approval does not

Feelings of regret, remorse, emptiness, guilt

Intensified need to assuage negative feelings

The Bible calls this cycle *envy*. It warns us that a life measured by possessions, particularly the possessions of our neighbors, is no life at all. It warns
us that coveting becomes a rottenness in our bones that eats away at peace
and contentment.

Enough = Fiscal Responsibility

Some of us have mastered our greed and are not driven hither and yon by
material desires. Some of us have risen above envy and no longer try to keep
up with the Joneses. We, instead, define "enough" as responsibly managing
the money at our disposal.

We limit our expenditures to income. We make do. We drive used cars.
We live in modest houses. We've downsized and simplified. We refuse to
go into debt. We've cut up our credit cards. We have the equivalent of three
months' salary in savings. We are invested in property, stocks, annuities,
401(k)s. We are diversified. We are preparing a financial future by exercising
financial discipline in our material present.

We've decided to be wise in the ways of money. And that's a good thing.
(At least, it's better than being *foolish* in the ways of money.) But if we are
not careful, we'll define good financial management as a form of godliness
when—in fact—it may be nothing more than building bigger barns.

Remember the Parable of the Rich Fool? (We talked about this story in
the previous chapter.) Jesus never accused the wealthy farmer of being grasp-
ingly greedy or endlessly envious. He spoke, instead, of a man who managed
his abundance in a disciplined manner—saving today to meet his needs
tomorrow. This fellow was wise in the ways of money.

But God still wasn't happy with him. Called him a fool, in fact. Claimed
that—in spite of his impressive barns—he wasn't wealthy where it counted.
The Parable of the Rich Fool suggests it is possible to be wise in the ways of
money and foolish about the ways of God.

There is a certain kind of Christian who confuses fiscal responsibility
with godliness. Curb your urge. Live within your means. Save for tomorrow.
And God will be pleased.

People caught in this thinking, however, often make a fatal mistake. In
their obsession with wise money management, they forget the point of that

management. They congratulate themselves for their abundance and then promptly invest that abundance in themselves, their own purposes and plans, their personal futures. They forget the kingdom and focus on their barns.

Focus on managing money wisely

Value being rich above being rich toward God

Save, accumulate, and invest—live free of debt or financial dependence

Manage your resources without reference to God's kingdom and God's will

Question: What should you do with your abundance?

Build bigger barns

Answer: Store up for yourself and your needs

God doesn't share his blessings with us so we can highjack those blessings for our own purposes and plans—however wisely we might manage those blessings in the meantime. God gives us his blessings in hopes that we will use those blessings to further his purposes. Yes, God wants to provide for us and our material needs. But that is not his *only* purpose. It is certainly not his *primary* purpose. Material resources, used without reference to God and his kingdom, are a *misuse* of resources no matter how well managed they may be.

The Bible does not refer to such misuse as greed or envy. It labels this misappropriation *foolishness* and warns that God will not overlook such folly. Perhaps you regard foolishness as a lesser sin than greed or envy. Perhaps you'd rather be thought a fool than avaricious or covetous. But the end is the same: putting things before God . . . forgetting where blessings come from and why they are given . . . ignoring God's will and work . . . valuing your priorities above his.

Enough = Creating a Margin for Generosity

Perhaps the real answer to the question "How much is enough?" is a commitment to generosity—whatever the quantity of possessions you may have

accumulated, whether you have much or little. Perhaps the trick is discon-
necting "enough" from possessions entirely and answering with *who we are*
rather than what we have.

For those Christians who really "get it" where the teachings of Jesus are
concerned, "enough" is the ability to take care of oneself *and* show generosity.
"Enough" is having sufficient resources to share with others.

Imagine living with a constant sense of gratitude to God. Imagine translating that gratitude into compassion. And imagine expressing compassion
in generous, unstinting, open-handed gifts of mercy. That's what happens in
the lives of people who realize that generosity is not a virtue lurking at the
periphery of Christian living. It is a core value, built into the coding of our
Christian DNA. Generosity is not a luxury, a take-it-or-leave-it option in the
life of a disciple. It is the purest expression of our discipleship.

Sadly, many of us have no margin for generosity. We couldn't share if we
wanted to. We are overcommitted, in debt, mortgaged to the hilt, and scram-
bling to cover our payments. Many of us live right at the ragged edge financially. We spend what we earn (and *then* some). There is little left at the end
of the month for generosity.

Focus on the
kingdom

Be content with
what God provides

Live frugally so you have a
margin for generosity

Trust God to provide for
your every need

Look for opportunities
to do good

Share your possessions for
kingdom purposes

To create a margin for generosity requires us to think intentionally about
our resources. Do we value generosity enough to dial back our standard of
living, to ensure our expenses are lower than our income? Will we live frugally enough to allow a financial buffer that can be focused on the needs of
others? Will we be aware of people in need, of causes worth supporting, of

opportunities to be generous? And will we learn the secret of contentment about the finite material resources we have at our disposal?

This will require us to redefine "enough." "Enough" isn't about what we want or what others have or even responsible fiscal management. "Enough" is learning to live within our means to such an extent that we have a margin—the financial leeway—to be generous when given the chance.

Watch Out for the Weeds

Satan wants to snatch faith from our hearts—he's just looking for his chance. Tomorrow, some awful tragedy may fall on one of us and burn away our hope. Frankly, you and I don't have a great deal of control over such matters.

But we can watch out for the weeds. We can guard against a love of things, the motives of the material, the worries of money—thorns that worm their way into our hearts and crowd out the commitments that count. We can refuse to be led around by our desires or the material ambitions of our peers. We can refrain from confusing good management with godly motives.

And we can make a commitment to generosity, to recognize that God has blessed us so that we bless others.

Exercises

1. What do your credit cards (or your level of indebtedness) tell you about your personal definition of "enough"?
2. How is your standard of living different from your parents? From your friends and peers? From the standard of living your children might experience?
3. Do your things own you?
4. Would you ever be tempted to equate financial responsibility with godliness?
5. What are the weeds in your life that you might need to root out?
6. How are you using what God has given you to bless other people? What is your margin for generosity?

Note

1. Matthew 13:24–30.

APPENDICES

In most books, appendices are reserved for content that isn't important enough to go into the body of the book itself but—on the other hand—
cannot be excluded altogether. Like footnotes, appendices are a necessary
evil. They are the "broccoli" of the book world: good for you in the long run
but difficult to chew, swallow, and digest.

That may be true of most books. But not this one.

The material in the following appendices is some of the most important
and practical content in all the pages of *Leaving a Legacy*. The exercises found
here provide the practical tools for turning pretty principles into applied

practice. Think of this material as the juncture at which the rubber of legacy meets the road of your life and family.

The chapters of *Leaving a Legacy* have introduced you to some important concepts: the primacy of legacy over inheritance . . . the Ninety Percent Rule . . . the need for intentionality and planning . . . the Legacy Process . . . a theology of possessions. But concepts don't have much personal value until they are applied. And the exercises included in these appendices are meant to apply the concepts of *Leaving a Legacy* to your family, to make a tangible difference for your family's future.

So don't leave these appendices languishing in lonely disregard. Don't assume these exercises are "after thoughts," banished to the back of the book because they are less worthy. We put this material in appendices because the flow of the chapters demanded it. Exercises are hard on reading. They make it difficult for readers to "stay on point" by intruding every few pages and demanding attention and participation.

But the chapters without the appendices are theories without implementation, empty calories devoid of the protein and vitamins that make for a healthy meal. Read the chapters, certainly. But then turn to these appendices and do the exercises. It's one of the best ways to turn "intentions into intentionality."

For those who are interested, there is also a workbook version of these (and other) exercises. You can download a PDF version of the workbook at: www.garrettgroupinc.com/legacyworkbook or www.theacufoundation.org/legacyworkbook.

JESUS ON POSSESSIONS AND MATERIAL WEALTH

When you give to the needy, do not let your left hand know what your right hand is doing, so that your giving may be in secret. (Matthew 6:3–4)

Give us today our daily bread. (Matthew 6:11 and Luke 11:3)

Do not store up for yourselves treasures on earth, where moths and vermin destroy, and where thieves break in and steal. But store up for yourselves treasures in heaven, where moths and vermin do not destroy, and where thieves do not break in and steal. (Matthew 6:19–20)

For where your treasure is, there your heart will be also. (Matthew 6:21 and Luke 12:34)

You cannot serve both God and money. (Matthew 6:24 and Luke 16:13)

Do not worry about your life, what you will eat or drink; or about your body, what you will wear. Is not life more than food, and the body more than clothes? (Matthew 6:25 and Luke 12:22–23)

Do not worry, saying, "What shall we eat?" or "What shall we drink?" or "What shall we wear?" For the pagans run after all these things, and your heavenly Father knows that you need them. But seek first his kingdom and his righteousness, and all these things will be given to you as well. (Matthew 6:31–33 and Luke 12:29–31)

If you, then, though you are evil, know how to give good gifts to your children, how much more will your Father in heaven give good gifts to those who ask him! (Matthew 7:11 and Luke 11:13)

Foxes have dens and birds have nests, but the Son of Man has no place to lay his head. (Matthew 8:20 and Luke 9:58)

Do not get any gold or silver or copper to take with you in your belts— no bag for the journey or extra shirt or sandals or a staff, for the worker is worth his keep. (Matthew 10:9–10 and Mark 6:8; Luke 9:3; Luke 10:4)

If any of you has a sheep and it falls into a pit on the Sabbath, will you not take hold of it and lift it out? How much more valuable is a person than a sheep! Therefore it is lawful to do good on the Sabbath. (Matthew 12:11–12)

The kingdom of heaven is like treasure hidden in a field. When a man found it, he hid it again, and then in his joy went and sold all he had and bought that field. (Matthew 13:44)

Again, the kingdom of heaven is like a merchant looking for fine pearls. When he found one of great value, he went away and sold everything he had and bought it. (Matthew 13:45–46)

What good will it be for someone to gain the whole world, yet forfeit their soul? Or what can anyone give in exchange for their soul? (Matthew 16:26 and Mark 8:36; Luke 9:25)

Truly I tell you, it is hard for someone who is rich to enter the kingdom of heaven. Again I tell you, it is easier for a camel to go through the eye of a needle than for someone who is rich to enter the kingdom of God. (Matthew 19:23–24 and Mark 10:23–25)

Everyone who has left houses or brothers or sisters or father or mother or wife or children or fields for my sake will receive a hundred times as much and will inherit eternal life. (Matthew 19:29, Mark 10:29–30, and Luke 18:29–30)

Jesus entered the temple courts and drove out all who were buying and selling there. He overturned the tables of the money changers and the benches of those selling doves. "It is written," he said to them, "'My house will be called a house of prayer,' but you are making it 'a den of robbers.'" (Matthew 21:12–13)

Give back to Caesar what is Caesar's, and to God what is God's. (Matthew 22:21, Mark 12:17, and Luke 20:25)

You say, "If anyone swears by the temple, it means nothing; but anyone who swears by the gold of the temple is bound by that oath." You blind fools! Which is greater: the gold, or the temple that makes the gold sacred? (Matthew 23:16–17)

You also say, "If anyone swears by the altar, it means nothing; but anyone who swears by the gift on the altar is bound by that oath." You blind men! Which is greater: the gift, or the altar that makes the gift sacred? (Matthew 23:18–19)

You give a tenth of your spices—mint, dill and cumin. But you have neglected the more important matters of the law—justice, mercy and faithfulness. (Matthew 23:23; Luke 11:42)

A woman came to him with an alabaster jar of very expensive perfume, which she poured on his head as he was reclining at the table. When the disciples saw this, they were indignant. "Why this waste?" they asked. "This perfume could have been sold at a high price and the money given to the poor." Aware of this, Jesus said to them, "Why are you bothering this woman? She has done a beautiful thing to me. The poor you will always have with you, but you will not always have me. (Matthew 26:7–11; Mark 14:7; John 12:8)

The worries of this life, the deceitfulness of wealth and the desires for other things come in and choke the word, making it unfruitful. (Mark 4:19 and Matthew 13:22; Luke 8:14)

This poor widow has put more into the treasury than all the others. They all gave out of their wealth; but she, out of her poverty, put in everything—all she had to live on. (Mark 12:43–44 and Luke 21:3–4)

Blessed are you who are poor, for yours is the kingdom of God.

Blessed are you who hunger now, for you will be satisfied. (Luke 6:20–21)

But woe to you who are rich, for you have already received your comfort. Woe to you who are well fed now, for you will go hungry. (Luke 6:24–25)

Give to everyone who asks you, and if anyone takes what belongs to you, do not demand it back. (Luke 6:30)

If you lend to those from whom you expect repayment, what credit is that to you? Even sinners lend to sinners, expecting to be repaid in full. But love your enemies, do good to them, and lend to them without expecting to get anything back. Then your reward will be great, and you will be children of the Most High, because he is kind to the ungrateful and wicked. (Luke 6:34–35)

Give, and it will be given to you. A good measure, pressed down, shaken together and running over, will be poured into your lap. For with the measure you use, it will be measured to you. (Luke 6:38)

Watch out! Be on your guard against all kinds of greed; life does not consist in an abundance of possessions. (Luke 12:15)

Sell your possessions and give to the poor. Provide purses for yourselves that will not wear out, a treasure in heaven that will never fail. (Luke 12:33)

Those of you who do not give up everything you have cannot be my disciples. (Luke 14:33)

Use worldly wealth to gain friends for yourselves, so that when it is gone, you will be welcomed into eternal dwellings. (Luke 16:9)

Whoever can be trusted with very little can also be trusted with much, and whoever is dishonest with very little will also be dishonest with much. So if you have not been trustworthy in handling worldly wealth, who will trust you with true riches? And if you have not been trustworthy with someone else's property, who will give you property of your own? (Luke 16:10–12)

What people value highly is detestable in God's sight. (Luke 16:15)

Stop turning my Father's house into a market! (John 2:16)

CHAPTER THREE EXERCISES

My Heirs

Consider the relationships listed in the table below, relationships you have cultivated over a lifetime. Who are you connected to? Whose life is tied up with your own?

It is important to list *specific people* and not simply deal in *general categories*. So if you have several children, list them by name. Four or five close friends? Write them down. Spiritual mentors? Who were they?

Not all of your prized relationships are "interpersonal." You also have relationships with certain charities, causes, ministries, and so on. These mean a great deal to you. You have invested in them, worked hard to manage and grow them, given generously to them. List them.

In the table below, write out the names of specific people and groups with whom you have built meaningful and treasured relationships.

Relationship	Specific Names
Spouse	
Children	

Members of your extended family	
Close friends	
Grandchildren/descendants	
Significant mentors/teachers	
Spiritual family (people and places who have nurtured you spiritually)	
Business relationships (associates, partners, companies you are connected to)	
Institutions (charities, ministries, and causes you have invested in)	
Other	

My Gifts

The table lists a few of the "gifts" you might consider passing on to your loved ones. Focus, first, on the left-hand column. Think about each item. Spend a little time meditating and praying over the nature of each characteristic or attitude or habit. Do you see the benefit and value of these things? Do you begin to see how much broader and deeper your legacy is than mere money?

Once you've finished naming a gift for each category, spend some time considering their relative importance. The middle column asks you to "Rank the importance of these gifts to *you*." Which of these things has meant the most to you? Which, do you believe, would make the most difference to the lives of those you love? Not all of them carry equal weight. Finding a *hobby* is a good thing, but demonstrating *integrity* is critical (as an example). As you think about your heirs, what are the top three gifts you would like to see them receive from you? How does a financial bequest rate with the other gifts you want to pass on?

Do your heirs agree? (Look at the right-hand column.) Do they value these gifts as you do? Which of these gifts do you think is most important *to them*? How would they rank these matters? Are they most interested in their financial inheritance or in an inheritance measured in character, competencies, and life lessons?

Type of Bequest This exercise represents some preliminary thinking about the nature of your gifts to the future. The purpose here is not to be *exhaustive* or *comprehensive* but to recognize that your legacy is greater than material resources. Try to list *one thing* for each of the categories below.	Rank the importance of these gifts to you	Rank the importance of these gifts to your heirs
What financial or material gifts do you have to offer your heirs?		
What is one relationships skill you possess that you would like to pass along to others (e.g., kindness, generosity, forgiveness, encouragement)?		
Name one emotional characteristic you possess that you would like to give your heirs (e.g., joy, stability, fearlessness, maturity).		
What is one character trait you evidence that you would like to pass along (e.g., loyalty, perseverance, honesty, mercy, sense of humor)?		
List one intellectual characteristic you possess that would benefit your heirs (e.g., curiosity, the habit of reading, being a lifelong learner).		
Identify a spiritual habit you've developed that you would commend to your children (e.g., prayer, Bible reading, commitment to ministry, church).		
Write down a favorite proverb for living that has served you well and would benefit your heirs (e.g., "Seek wisdom" or "Carpe diem").		
What is one family tradition you would like your heirs to remember and celebrate (e.g., Thanksgiving dinner, Family Night, birthday bashes)?		
Is there one core value that has benefited you and would greatly benefit your heirs (e.g., work hard, family first, keep your word, stay positive)?		
Name one habit that has served you well and would bless your heirs (e.g., physical fitness, tithing, rest, meditation, reading).		
Have you learned the power of gratitude, encouragement, and affirmation? • To whom do you need to say "Thank you"? • Who would benefit most by a word of encouragement from you? • Which of your loved ones needs your affirmation?		
What is one genetic inheritance your children have received from you (e.g., longevity, health, intelligence, good teeth, leadership)?		

What one thing have you learned about friendship that you would like your heirs to learn (e.g., friends are few and precious, be a friend and you'll have friends, friends are worth the investment)?		
Is there one cause you have championed that you would like to see your heirs adopt and advocate?		
Name one hobby that has given you great joy and that you would commend to your heirs (e.g., music, fishing, knitting, woodworking).		

Who Gets What from Me?

Give to everyone what you owe them: If you owe taxes, pay taxes; if revenue, then revenue; if respect, then respect; if honor, then honor. (Romans 13:7)

Match the "who" with the "what." You have certain gifts to give. You also have certain people you love. Not everyone gets the same gifts. What gifts would you like your children to receive from you? Your friends? The causes to which you have dedicated your life?

The first exercise of this chapter (*My Heirs*) asked you to specifically name the network of meaningful relationships you've developed over the course of your life. Use that exercise to expand the list of relationships in the table below.

This checklist will help you recognize the range of debts you owe to a range of people. It will help you define "heir" by more than genetics. It will help you define "gift" by more than finances. And it will give you a head start toward giving "everyone what you owe them" while you still have breath to do so.

Gifts	Material possessions	People skills	Emotional IQ	Character traits	Intellectual traits	Spiritual habits	Life lessons	Family traditions	Core values	Habits	Gratitude	Encouragement	Affirmation	Genetic inheritance	Friendships/mentors	Commitment to cause	Hobby/joie de vivre
Relationship																	
Spouse																	
Children																	
Extended family																	
Close friends																	
Mentors/teachers																	
Neighbors																	
Spiritual family																	
Business associates																	
Institutions																	
Other																	

My Tools

Using the table below, match the tool with the task. Just as you wouldn't use a chain saw to sand a plank of wood, so you wouldn't use just any of the available legacy tools to accomplish every legacy task. Some tools are more suitable for the need.

If, for instance, you hope to pass on a legacy of generosity or integrity or compassion to the loved ones you leave behind, a legal will cannot accomplish that. Instead, you may need to tell some stories about the importance of compassion (from the Bible or from family history), have a conversation (or three) with your children about integrity, or involve your heirs in generously supporting a cause that is close to your heart.

Which tools are best suited for passing on a variety of legacy gifts? As you match them up, ask yourself which of those tools you are currently using. A will is necessary but not sufficient. There are some conversations you need to have, some encouragement you need to give, and some causes you need to promote with your loved ones.

Legacy Task / Tools	Material possessions	People skills	Emotional IQ	Character traits	Intellectual traits	Spiritual habits	Life lessons	Family traditions	Core values	Habits	Gratitude	Encouragement	Affirmation	Genetic inheritance	Friendships/mentors	Commitment to cause	Hobby/joie de vivre
Will/estate plan																	
Family stories																	
Bible stories																	
Proverbs/sayings																	
Confessions																	
Mission statement																	
Sharing life lessons																	
Personal example																	
Conversations																	
Testimonial/faith																	
Holding up heroes																	
Books/biographies																	
Compliments																	
Mementos																	

Documents/ lists														
Travel														
Philanthropy														
Other														

My Motives

There are many reasons for wanting to leave a legacy. The table below will help you identify a few that are significant for you. Don't breeze through this exercise thoughtlessly.

In the second column, you are invited to indicate which of the motives apply to you. Check any of the statements that reflect your thinking (even if it's a little embarrassing to admit). Then, in the third column, rank these motives in the order of their significance for you . . . the reasons you are motivated to pass something of significance to others.

Motivation	True of you?	Rank by significance to you
You can't take it with you		
Easy come, easy go		
They can figure it out on their own		
It's all vanity and vexation in the end		
I have nothing of importance to pass on		
I fear my legacy will involve more negatives than positives		
I love my family (wife, children, friends)		
I've learned some lessons worth passing on		
I believe there are truths that transcend any individual life		
I want to honor God		
I've learned there are values and character traits that lead to a happier life		
I want to be remembered after I'm gone		
I want to control my heirs, even from the grave		

If I don't set conditions and boundaries in my will, my kids are lost		
Our family has traditions worth keeping		
More than anything, I want my kids to be happy		
More than anything, I want my kids to have an active faith		
Nothing I do at the end will undo the damage I've done throughout my life		
I don't want the government to take what I've earned		
I want to perpetuate my projects and priorities through my heirs		
I want my heirs to do better, accomplish more, dream greater than I did		
My family needs to give itself to a cause greater than itself		
I have some wisdom I'd like to pass on to the future		
My family's name and reputation means everything to me		
Other		

LEGACY PLANNING ASSESSMENT

The assessment questions in this exercise have no right or wrong answers. There is no perfect response to these questions. They are designed to clarify your understanding of how well the significant people in your life are prepared to accept the greatest gifts you hope to give them at your death. They are designed to help you assess how well your heirs will handle your gifts after you are gone.

You don't have to answer every question. Some may not apply to you. But answer as many questions as are relevant to your situation.

Please respond to the questions by placing a number between 1 and 5 in the left-hand column.

1 = I haven't even started . . . I don't have a clue . . . not at all.

2 = I've just begun . . . I'm in the initial phases . . . I've communicated the basics.

3 = I've done some good work here, but I still have a way to go.

4 = I'm feeling pretty good about where I am with this.

5 = I'm finished and up-to-date . . . accomplished.

Response	Question
	1. Have you identified your heirs? (See *My Heirs* exercise in Appendix B.)
	2. How far along are you in your traditional estate planning? (Including legal documents such as will, power of attorney, trusts, life insurance policies, etc.)
	3. Are the documents related to this estate plan being kept up-to-date to reflect changes in your life and circumstances?
	4. Can your spouse and other heirs easily access that information? Do they know where the documents are kept or who to contact in the event of your death?
	5. Have you had in-depth conversations with your *spouse/executor* about the contents and design of your estate planning documents?
	6. Have you had in-depth conversations with your *children* and other significant heirs about the contents and design of your estate planning documents?
	7. Have you clarified long-term plans and hopes (i.e., legacy) for your family beyond the distribution of financial assets? (See the *My Gifts* exercise.)
	8. Have you communicated your legacy hopes and plans for your family to your *spouse*?
	9. Have you communicated your legacy hopes and plans for your family to your *children* and other significant heirs?
	10. Do your legal and financial advisors know about your larger legacy plans and hopes for your family? Do they understand them well enough to communicate these to your heirs?
	11. Have your advisors (attorney, CPA, financial planner/advisor, charitable gift planner) worked together (as a team) so that they know their various roles in carrying out your long-term wishes?
	12. If you own a business with a partner, do you have confidence that—in your absence—your partner will employ the kinds of values and ethics in his or her decision making about the future that you would have used?
	13. If you own a business with a partner, have you discussed with your spouse and heirs how comfortable they would be that—in your absence—your partner will treat them with respect and honesty?
	14. If so, did your spouse and heirs give the response you expected about their level of comfort with your business partner?
	15. Have you communicated to your children and other heirs the story of how you accumulated your wealth?
	16. Have you shared that story with your heirs in any *formal* way (family meetings, video or audio recording, written story, etc.)?
	17. Have you communicated to your children and other heirs the history and heritage of your family? (See the *Family* section of Chapter Seven.)
	18. Have you written a personal vision statement? (Can your spouse and other heirs easily access that information?)
	19. Have you written a family vision statement? (See Chapter Eight.) (Can your spouse and other heirs easily access that information?)

	20. Have you written out your personal statement of faith? A "testimonial" of what faith means to you? (See the *My Faith* exercise in Chapter Seven.) (Can your spouse and other heirs easily access that information?)
	21. Have you talked to your family, heirs, and advisors about the people who have formed your most significant relationships—friends, mentors, spiritual influences? (See Chapter Three.)
	22. Have you talked to your family, heirs, and advisors about the institutions and charities you have supported and championed through your life? Have you told them why these institutions and charities mean so much to you? (See Chapter Three.)
	23. Have you had significant conversations with your family, heirs, and advisors about the values and traits that you held most closely in your life? (See the *My Gifts* exercise in Chapter Three. More on this in Chapters Seven and Eight.)
	24. Have you determined whether your family, heirs, and advisors share those values and traits with you?
	25. Have you talked to your family and heirs about what you hope to pass on to each of them—which parts of your legacy you hope they will inherit from you? (See *Who Gets What from Me?* in Chapter Three.)
	26. Have you identified the family traditions you hold dear and hope will continue? (See the *Family* section of Chapter Seven.)
	27. Have you identified the life lessons, proverbs, or maxims that have proven most valuable in your life and commended them to your children or heirs? (See the *Life Lessons* exercise in Chapter Seven.)
	28. Have you developed and used the various tools (described in *My Tools* in Chapter Three) for communicating and inculcating the values that mean most to you?
	29. Have you told your family and heirs why it is so important to you to pass along more than just money? Why you are motivated to pass on a legacy? (See the *My Motives* exercise in Chapter Three.)
	30. If your oldest child were shown your responses to the *My Gifts* exercise (in Chapter Three), would he or she recognize the values you indicated as most important to you?
	31. Would your second child recognize those values?
	32. Would your third child recognize those values?
	33. Would your fourth child recognize those values?
	34. Would your fifth child recognize those values? (etc.)
	35. If your oldest child were shown your responses to the *My Gifts* exercise, how aligned would his or her values be with yours?
	36. Would your second child's values be aligned with your own?
	37. Would your third child's values be aligned with your own?
	38. Would your fourth child's values be aligned with your own?
	39. Would your fifth child's values be aligned with your own? (etc.)

	40. Have you determined and communicated how important it is for your children to understand the relationship between the values you embraced and the success you enjoyed?
	41. Have you determined and communicated that it is just as important for your children to understand the relationship between values and success as it is for them to understand the terms and conditions of the estate planning documents with which your assets will be distributed?
	42. Have you considered, prayed about, and communicated the role a financial inheritance from you is expected to play in helping your heirs live healthier, fuller, and more productive lives?
	Sum: Add up the numbers you provided in the left-hand column.
	Count: Tally the number of questions you answered.
	Divide: Find your average response by dividing the Sum by the Count.

This is not a test. It is simply an exercise to help you become better acquainted with your feelings, attitudes, and actions in planning for the future and preparing your heirs for that future.

- If you *sum* the responses you gave and *divide* it by the number of questions you answered, you will get an *average* score per answer.
- Since this is not a test, what is important to determine here is not your *score* ("I got a 2.5788!") but your *tendency* (well prepared . . . poorly prepared . . . somewhere in the middle).

If your average score was 4 or better, you have done a remarkable job of communicating with your family about what matters most to you in life . . . about what you hope will matter most to them. Your heirs should have a crystal-clear understanding of what they need to do when you die, what they should expect as an inheritance, and the scope of the larger legacy you hope to place into their hands.

On the other hand, if your average score was less than 3 (and, particularly, if it was *significantly* less!), it's time to get out the picks and shovels and begin laying a personal-planning foundation. It's time to count the cost, devote the resources, and commit to a plan for building the tower of your legacy.

CHAPTER SEVEN EXERCISES

Our Family Tree

The journey to legacy begins by telling the story of your heritage. Take out a sheet of paper (actually, you might want to purchase a nice journal and keep all your legacy notes there!) and fill in names on the following chart.

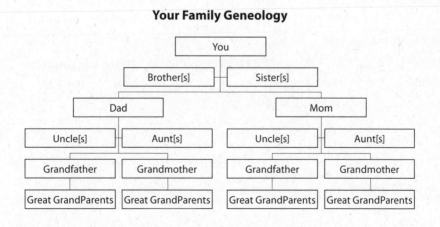

Your Family Geneology

211

Make this genealogical chart as detailed as you want: nieces and nephews, cousins, and so on. If you know the names of great-great-grandparents, wonderful. If you can attach dates, excellent. If you have any facts to add— significant accomplishments, educational attainments, founding of businesses—better still. Best of all, if you can attach photos, birth certificates, or other documentation to each name, that would be super.

Our Heritage

Take out a sheet (or three) of paper and jot down your answers to the following questions about your family of origin. Don't think too hard about your answers. Don't get bogged down. Write out the first thoughts that come to mind. You can fill in the details later.

1. Describe the home and family you grew up in.
2. Describe your relationship with your parents.
3. What were the characteristics you most admired in your parents?
4. How do you remember them spending time with you?
5. How did you spend "family" time in the home in your family of origin?
6. When your parents talked about "family characteristics," what traits would they mention? What does it mean to be a [your surname]?
7. What were the most significant traditions/characteristic activities in which you participated in your family of origin (e.g., Christmas rituals, fishing, travel)?
8. What were your family's priorities growing up?
9. How did your family (parents) define "success" as you were growing up?
10. What is the ethnic/national/cultural background of your family?
11. How well did you know your grandparents?

12. What are your most significant memories of your grandparents?
13. What were the characteristics you saw in your grandparents?
14. What are the "family stories" you heard (and told) about your family/ancestors?
15. What is the meaning of your family name? Where did it come from?
16. Thinking back over the past few generations, who was the "golden child" of your family? Who was the "black sheep"?
17. What kinds of work did your ancestors do? Do you have a blue-collar or white-collar background? Were your ancestors farmers or bankers or plumbers or entrepreneurs?
18. What were your extended family's attitudes about religion, education, politics?

More sheets of paper. Answer some questions about yourself in light of your family of origin.

1. What one virtue did you "inherit" that came directly from your parents/family?
2. What one vice did you "inherit" that came directly from your parents/family?
3. Which of your family members do you most take after? Who do you most resemble (for people who know your family well)?
4. Describe a couple of significant family experiences that affected or shaped you in your formative years.
5. Are you proud of/ashamed about/indifferent to being a [your surname]?
6. How did your family of origin most shape the person you are today?
7. How has the ethnic/cultural background of your family influenced you?
8. If you were to name a couple of lessons you learned growing up in your family, what would they be?

9. On a scale of 1 to 10, where did (or do) relationships with members of your extended family rate in your life?

Our Immediate Family

Focus on your spouse and children. Write some thoughtful responses to the following questions:

1. How did you and your spouse meet?
2. Describe your dating life.
3. When and why did you decide to marry?
4. What would you identify as the "great strength" of your marriage?
5. What would you identify as the "great challenge" of your marriage?
6. In what significant ways does your own marriage reflect that of your parents?
7. In what significant ways is your own marriage different from that of your parents?
8. What are your first memories of each of your children?
9. Describe the personalities, talents, and traits of each of your children.
10. How connected are your children to your extended family? Do your children have a sense of being [your surname]? Do they understand what that means?
11. How did (or do) the priorities of your family of origin impact your immediate family?
12. How is your own family significantly different from your family of origin?
13. What are the values/lessons/characteristics you would most like your children to inherit from your family of origin?
14. Have your children adopted the traditions/activities of your family of origin?

15. Do your children appreciate their ethnic/cultural inheritance? Does it mean anything to them?
16. Have your children heard the stories of your ancestors/family?
17. What would you identify as the most significant impediments to strengthening your family relationships?
18. On a scale of 1 to 10, where do relationships with members of your immediate family rate in your life?

My Faith

Reflect on and respond to the following questions and prompts.

1. Write out a brief, personal "statement of faith."
2. How long (and in what way) have you considered yourself a "spiritual" person?
3. Did you grow up in church? Describe some early church experiences.
4. How and when did you make a commitment to follow God's will?
5. What is your most precious, treasured spiritual experience?
6. Who would you identify as important spiritual influences in your life?
7. Describe one instance where faith really made a difference for you.
8. What is your favorite Bible verse/story/theme? Explain why this means so much to you.
9. Is there a particular spiritual discipline that was especially meaningful to you (e.g., prayer, Bible reading, fasting, service, generosity, silence)?
10. Has God answered your prayers? Has he been faithful to you? How do you see that?
11. Did your parents pass on their faith to you? In what ways does your faith differ from that of your parents? How is it the same?

12. How did your family practice faith?

 ❑ Family devotionals
 ❑ Bible reading/Bible stories
 ❑ Prayers at mealtimes and bedtime
 ❑ Church attendance
 ❑ Involvement in ministry
 ❑ Other:

13. Do you want to pass on faith to your children? Do you think you have been successful in doing so?
14. In what ways would you hope your children's faith differs from yours? How would you hope it is similar?
15. On a scale of 1 to 10, where does your faith rate in importance to you?
16. Do your children know what your faith means to you?

Which of the following Scriptures would you recommend as a basic "guide for living" to your children? (OK, you can select two if you must!)

❑ "Love the Lord your God with all your heart and with all your soul and with all your strength and with all your mind"; and, "Love your neighbor as yourself." (Luke 10:27)

❑ So I commend the enjoyment of life, because there is nothing better for a person under the sun than to eat and drink and be glad. (Ecclesiastes 8:15)

❑ What good will it be for someone to gain the whole world, yet forfeit their soul? Or what can anyone give in exchange for their soul? (Matthew 16:26)

❑ Now all has been heard; here is the conclusion of the matter: Fear God and keep his commandments, for this is the duty of all mankind. (Ecclesiastes 12:13)

❑ In the same way, count yourselves dead to sin but alive to God in Christ Jesus. (Romans 6:11)

❑ It is by grace you have been saved, through faith—and this is not from yourselves, it is the gift of God. (Ephesians 2:8)

❑ Do not think of yourself more highly than you ought, but rather think of yourself with sober judgment, in accordance with the faith God has distributed to each of you. (Romans 12:3)

❑ Do not forsake wisdom, and she will protect you; love her, and she will watch over you. (Proverbs 4:6)

❑ Watch out! Be on your guard against all kinds of greed; life does not consist in an abundance of possessions. (Luke 12:15)

❑ Let us not love with words or speech but with actions and in truth. (1 John 3:18)

Which of the following godly virtues do you believe to be most important for building a successful life? (This chart is based on Galatians 5:21–22 and 2 Peter 1:5–7.)

❑ Love	❑ Patience	❑ Faithfulness
❑ Joy	❑ Kindness	❑ Gentleness
❑ Peace	❑ Goodness	❑ Self-control
❑ Knowledge	❑ Perseverance	❑ Godliness
❑ Friendliness	❑ Love	❑ Faith

My Life Lessons

1. What was the hardest life lesson you ever learned?
2. Is there one lesson you have learned about life (from your own living or from others) that you would recommend to your children?
3. Who would you point to (within your family or outside) as best exemplifying the quality or characteristic you would like to see in your children and grandchildren?
4. Have you talked to your children about these matters?
5. On a scale of 1 to 10, how valuable are these life lessons compared to the other things you want your children to inherit from you?

My Successes and Setbacks

Into every life, the sun will shine and the rain will fall. No life is devoid of achievement or immune to disappointments. It is how we handle the ebb and flow of life that determines how well we live. What would you want your heirs to know about managing whatever life may throw at them?

1. What would you identify as your single greatest success or accomplishment?
2. What characteristic or factor was most responsible for your success?
3. What was the most significant result of that success?
4. How did you celebrate that success?
5. Did that success or accomplishment make you vulnerable to future failures? How?
6. What lessons did you learn from this success or accomplishment?
7. What would you identify as your single greatest failure?
8. What factor or characteristic was most responsible for this failure?
9. What was the most significant result of this disappointment?
10. How did you handle this defeat?
11. What did you learn about persistence and perseverance through this experience?
12. Did that failure open doors to future successes or accomplishments? How?
13. What lessons did you learn from this disappointment?
14. If you had to choose, which taught you the most significant lessons about living: your successes or your failures?
15. What would you like your children and grandchildren to know about success?
16. What would you like your children and grandchildren to know about failure?

My Mentors

Who were the "influencers" in your life? The people who taught you about living? Do you know the people who shaped you? Do they know the pivotal role they played in your life?

Your Mentors		
Area of Influence	**Most significant mentor in this area**	**Lesson you learned**
How to deal with people		
How to be emotionally mature		
How to be curious		
How to be spiritual		
How to view life		
How to manage people		
How to run a business		
How to handle finances		
How to value family history and traditions		
How to value faith history and traditions		
How to learn from life		
How to be a person of character		
How to develop and value good habits		
How to develop and express good attitudes		
How to love books and education		
How to make and nurture friendships		
How to develop and keep a sense of humor		
How to find and champion causes or convictions		
How to work hard		

How to appreciate music and the arts		
How to be generous		

My Character

There are aspects of your personality, qualities of your nature, that have significantly impacted your life. We tend to take these qualities for granted. Like breathing, we rarely think about the things that come naturally to us. These exercises are offered to help you become more conscious of the characteristics that have contributed to your life.

1. Which of these character traits are most characteristic of you? (Choose two or three. We've only included the more positive traits. You can list your other, more difficult qualities if you want.)

❑ Adventurous   ❑ Ambitious   ❑ Assertive
❑ Attentive   ❑ Authentic   ❑ Brave
❑ Calm   ❑ Candid   ❑ Capable
❑ Charismatic   ❑ Committed   ❑ Compassionate
❑ Consistent   ❑ Creative   ❑ Curious
❑ Determined   ❑ Diplomatic   ❑ Disciplined
❑ Easygoing   ❑ Effective   ❑ Empathetic
❑ Energetic/enthusiastic ❑ Ethical   ❑ Expressive
❑ Fair   ❑ Faithful   ❑ Flexible
❑ Friendly   ❑ Generous   ❑ Grateful
❑ Happy   ❑ Hard-working   ❑ Honest
❑ Humorous   ❑ Independent   ❑ Innovative
❑ Intelligent   ❑ Intimate   ❑ Joyful
❑ Knowledgeable   ❑ Leader   ❑ Listener
❑ Logical   ❑ Loving   ❑ Loyal
❑ Open-minded   ❑ Optimistic   ❑ Organized

❑ Patient   ❑ Peace-loving   ❑ Persistent

❑ Persuasive   ❑ Planner   ❑ Powerful

❑ Practical   ❑ Problem-solver   ❑ Productive

❑ Reliable   ❑ Resourceful   ❑ Responsible

❑ Self-confident   ❑ Sense of humor   ❑ Servant

❑ Sincere   ❑ Skillful   ❑ Spiritual

❑ Spontaneous   ❑ Stable   ❑ Strong

❑ Team player   ❑ Tactful   ❑ Trusting

❑ Trustworthy   ❑ Truthful   ❑ Warm

❑ Willing   ❑ Wise   ❑ Zealous

2. How have these self-identified characteristics contributed positively to your life? Give some examples.
3. Which of these traits might you wish were *more* characteristic of you? (List two or three.) Why?
4. Which traits do you acknowledge as being uncharacteristic of you? (List two or three.)
5. Which traits (characteristic of you or not) would you most commend to your children? Why?

Our Money

There is an old saw that states, "The two things you don't talk about in polite society are politics and religion." In families, the taboo subject would seem to be sex. But, in fact, people have the hardest time talking about money—in just about any setting. Even in the most intimate of families, it is difficult to talk specifically and plainly about income, expenses, savings, assets, and inheritances.

Here are a few questions to help you have the "money discussion" with your family.

1. What is your first memory of money? Where did you get it? How did you use it?
2. What was your first job? How much did you earn? What did you do with your first paycheck? How did you use the income from this job?
3. When did you establish your "financial independence" from your parents? What did that feel like?
4. How do you view money? Where does money fit in your priorities?
5. Do you live by a budget? Do you live "within your means"? Why?
6. Do you practice the habits of saving and investing? Why? For how long? To what extent?
7. Do you practice the habit of generosity? Why? To what extent?
8. Do you feel a sense of "stewardship" for money . . . the notion that the material wealth passing through your hands is yours to "manage," not to "own" . . . that wealth is meant to be used for higher purposes than personal comforts and agendas? Explain.
9. Have you discussed your finances with your children? To what extent?
10. Do your children know about your habits of saving, investing, and generosity? To what extent?
11. Have you done "estate planning" in the event of your death? To what extent? Do you have the documents in place that will be necessary to an orderly and efficient inheritance by your heirs (wills, trusts, conveyances, etc.)?
12. Have you discussed your inheritance plans with your heirs? To what extent?
13. Have you experienced any disappointments with your children's management of money? Their spending habits, for instance? Mismanagement of the funds available to them? Poor spending choices? Lack of savings?
14. What does "wealth" mean to your children? Do you know?

15. What are your children's financial strengths and weaknesses? Can you list them?
16. Name one principle you would like to teach your children and grandchildren about wealth.
17. What would you like for your children's material inheritance to achieve for them?
18. What would you want your children to understand your material wealth has achieved for you?
19. On a scale of 1 to 10, relative to the other matters we have explored in this chapter (family, faith, life learning), how valuable are the material possessions you want your children to inherit from you?
20. Relative to the other matters we have explored in this chapter, how valuable are material possessions to your children?

CHAPTER EIGHT EXERCISES

A Heritage Biography

The following might serve as an outline for your family story. *Included are some abbreviated examples to consider.*

Start with general information, if you know it: where your family name came from, your family's ethnic and national roots, when your ancestors came to this country, and where they settled.

Work your way down the family tree. List names and appropriate details about your extended family. Write a brief description (physical, psychological, spiritual) of your grandparents and parents.

Papa Sim was a tall, spare man, a farmer who believed in raising his children like he raised his corn—tall and straight, no weeds, stone fences at the boundaries. He was deeply religious and considered his family, his work, and his word to be an expression of his faith. He loved to read.

If you were brave enough to make some generalizations about your wider family:

- What would you consider to be "family" characteristics or virtues?
- What kinds of work did your ancestors most often do? (Were they laborers or managers? Outdoorsmen or office workers?)
- Are there any characteristic attitudes you would note about your family? (Die-hard Democrats? Valued education? Frugal? Churchgoing?)

Our family has always been known for its sense of humor. Dry. Quick. A little ribald. A woman stopped my great-uncle as he was mowing his yard one day and asked how much he charged. He said, "Depends on the yard, but this lady" (nodding toward the house) "lets me sleep with her." The woman drove off at great speed.

Are there any rituals or traditions that have long been characteristic of your family? Family rites or customs passed on from prior generations that you still maintain today (and would like to encourage for tomorrow)?

Thanksgiving has always been our most important family observance. More than Christmas or birthdays or anniversaries. We ate our Thanksgiving dinner (complete with all the traditional dishes) in the late afternoon. But at noon, we always had "Thanksgiving Tea"—a formal time when we dressed up, had tea and biscuits, and went around the table to talk about our year. When I was younger, this ritual (that traces back at least to my grandparents) was excruciating. The older I get, the more this time means to me . . . and moves me.

Are there any family stories, passed down by your parents or grandparents, you would like your children to know about? Any stories *about* your parents or grandparents they should hear?

My parents worked a small farm during the Depression. One of my strongest childhood memories involves needy strangers stopping by our door to ask for a meal. We didn't have much ourselves, but my mother always filled a plate and let these men eat on our back porch. Every time, she told us children, "A man is more than his circumstance."

My Autobiography

Consider the following outline for your personal story (including, again, some abbreviated examples).

Childhood: Where were you born? Where did you live as a child? What are your earliest memories? What are your most significant memories about your home . . . school . . . church, etc.? (Look over your notes for *Our Heritage*—at the end of Chapter Seven—as you think about your younger years and your family of origin.)

> *I was seven years old. We lived in Little Rock, Arkansas. The "Lone Ranger" was a popular TV show at the time—black and white, of course. I decided I had to have a cowboy outfit, complete with hat, boots, and six-gun. And I decided that God should give it to me. I prayed and prayed. And then I went looking in closets, behind doors, under beds. No outfit. Thirty-five years later, I told this story (and confessed my disappointment) in a sermon. The next week, a full cowboy outfit was delivered to my office, courtesy of a member of my church. God answers prayers in his own way and in his own time.*

Teen Years: What were you like as a teenager? Were you popular, athletic, bookish, awkward? What was your first job? Who was your first romance? What did you like to do? What is your most significant high school memory? How did your teen years shape the person you've become? How did you and your parents get along during that phase of your life?

> *I went to a very small high school—twenty-seven people in my graduating class. But the school had a great football program. Every able-bodied male was expected to play football. I went out for the team my senior year—all 140 pounds of me. They put me on the front line (a guard!). I spent the year getting pummeled by much larger and more athletic opponents. I wasn't very good—except at nursing bruises and strains. But, ever since, I haven't been afraid of squaring off against unlikely odds.*

Formative Influences: Identify a handful of key influences that shaped you in your younger years: family (including—where appropriate—grandparents, uncles and aunts, and siblings), travel, books, church, teachers/mentors, school, sports, helpful (or hurtful) experiences, work, and so on.

> *I struggled academically my first years in high school—failed Latin, barely passed most other classes. But an English teacher (Mrs. Lynn) took an active interest in me and encouraged my writing. I won a statewide essay contest as a junior. Her interest turned my life around. I've written a dozen books as an adult and, with each new book, I think about the debt I owe Mrs. Lynn.*

Dating and Marriage: When did you first meet your spouse? Describe your first date. What attracted you to him or her? What did you have in common? How did your relationship grow? Describe the decision to marry. What was life like in your early married years? What were your primary joys and struggles? (Review your notes on *Our Immediate Family* at the end of Chapter Seven.)

> *Our first date was dinner at a local seafood restaurant. Linen and crystal. I really splurged. Our second date was to McDonald's—a sign of things to come! There has been a lot more fast food than seafood over the years of our marriage. But I've always enjoyed the company, whatever the menu.*

Career: Trace the trajectory of your career over the years. Where did you start out? What kind of work did you do? How did your occupation evolve over time? Did you end up where you thought you would? How would you do things differently if you could start over? What lessons did your working life teach you?

> *I interviewed for a job in Texas when you kids were young. The position was prestigious and paid good money. But during the interview, I learned that my boss-to-be had very definite ideas about how to do my job, what my boundaries would be, and how my performance would be measured. I wanted to think outside the box; he wanted me in it. I wanted to push the envelope; he wanted me to lick it. I turned the job down.*

Our Family Story

Look through your notes on *Our Immediate Family* again as you prepare to describe:

Your Children: Where were your children born? What are your first memories of each child? How did you choose their names? What personality traits did you first notice (and continue to notice) in each of your children? What gifts or talents have you seen in them? What is one thing you are proudest of about each of them? If you had a crystal ball, what would you predict about their future? What is one way they are like you? What is one way they are different from you?

> *Sarah, the first time I held you was outside the delivery room. The nurse handed your little bundled body to me and instructed me to take you to the nursery. We had this quiet, magical moment in the hallway where I welcomed you into the world, told you our hopes for you, and apologized (in advance) for all the mistakes your mother and I were going to make. You smiled at me like you understood every word. Then you emptied your bladder and that magic moment ended! But there was so much magic yet to come.*

Your Family's Traditions, Rituals, and Hobbies: What did your family do on vacations? What hobbies and activities did you enjoy together? Are there particularly memorable moments from family travels or camping or movie nights or [fill in the blank] that the whole family cherishes? What are some of your family traditions (e.g., praying at meals, Christmas morning rituals, going to the ballpark on the first day of the season, attending church, Easter at Granny's)?

> *Each year at Christmas, we added a new, shiny, red ornament to our tree. We wrote a few memories from the year—notable achievements, major events—on the ornament in white ink. And we would read what we'd written on all the red ornaments from past years, adding them to the tree and remembering. As years passed, the "reading of the ornaments" got longer*

and longer. You kids came to dread that ritual. But I love it and hope that, in your own families, you might make room for that a ritual yourselves.

Your Family Values and Traits:
- What would you identify as the three most dominant *personality traits* that consistently run through your family? (You might want to review your notes on *My Character* at the conclusion of Chapter Seven.)
- How have these traits made a positive contribution to your family?
- Which of these traits do you see expressing themselves in each of your children? How?
- What would you identify as the three most dominant *values* that consistently run through your family (e.g., honesty, hard work, faith, open dialogue, independence, compassion)?

Our family loves to read. We come by it honestly, born of a long line of bibliophiles. Doesn't really matter what—fiction, history, biography, science . . . as long as we have a book in our hands (or, now, on our iPads). It is a source of secret pride to me that, when it comes time for you guys to move, the chief complaint is about the boxes of books you have to haul around.

A Checklist for Your Family Vision Statement

❑ A message to heirs explaining the purpose and importance of the Family Vision Statement

❑ A Heritage Biography summarizing the history of your extended family

❑ An Autobiography telling your personal story

❑ Our Family Story—a summary of the history and character of your immediate family

❑ A statement of faith and values—distilling wisdom from higher sources

❑ Character and Significance—a brief reflection on the traits and people who have shaped you and served you well

- ❏ A definition of wealth and the desired effects of inheritance on your children
- ❏ Financial objectives (what you hope inheritance can do for your children)
- ❏ Balancing—a legacy of generosity, not just possessions
- ❏ Introduction of the Family Retreat and Family Council

PLANNING DOCUMENTS CHECKLIST

❑ A list of *heirs* (identifying relationships that have defined and shaped your life).

❑ An initial look at the *gifts* you have to offer your family for the future (seeing and defining a legacy larger than possessions).

❑ An initial consideration of *what you owe* the people you love (recognizing the people you love need more from you than your money).

❑ An initial survey of your legacy *tool box* (affirming that there are many ways to skin the legacy cat!).

❑ A quick stab at admitting your *motives* for wanting to leave a legacy (answering the "Why bother?" question about the future).

❑ Paperwork that reflects the arrangements you've made with a *partner*, if you've asked someone to join you in this process (especially if you've identified an experienced facilitator and signed a working agreement).

❑ A *letter* (signed, sealed, but as yet undelivered) you've written to your great-great-grandchildren.

❑ The *Legacy Planning Assessment*, with which you have seen how prepared you are for passing on your valuables and your values. (You may still have plenty of work to make the preparations you want for your

family's future. That's OK. These preparations should become part of
your planning process.)

- ❑ Will
- ❑ Trust Documents
- ❑ Power of Attorney
- ❑ Insurance Policies
- ❑ Executor Documents
- ❑ Other:

- ❑ A *family tree*.
- ❑ Many pages of memories and musings, photographs and certificates,
  stories and traditions drawn from your *family heritage*. This is rich
  material, the true gold you've mined from the history of where you
  came from!
- ❑ Pages of memories, observations, and affirmations of your *immediate
  family*. Photos. Copies of birth certificates. Lists of family traditions.
  Good stuff!
- ❑ Reflections on the importance of *faith*. Your personal testimony.
- ❑ Reflections on the most *significant lessons* you've learned about life.
- ❑ Reflections on *successes and setbacks*.
- ❑ A list of your *mentors* and their areas of influence.
- ❑ Reflections on your *character traits*.
- ❑ Reflections on *money*: how you made it, where it fits in your scheme of
  priorities, and inheritance issues.
- ❑ Family Vision Statement.

NAVIGATOR
Legacy Partners, LLC

With over 80 years of team experience working with individuals and families, we have found that planning for the **future of your money** is not the same as planning for the **future of your family.**

Men and women of faith have often shared the burden they feel when they focus their heartfelt desire to be the best possible steward of the gifts they have received from God with us. We are asked, "What is the best way to develop and encourage our family so that our financial resources do not become a negative when our family receives them?" Unfortunately, there is not a one size fits all answer to this pressing question.

Navigator Legacy Partners, LLC helps families to:

- *Improve communication and trust and learn how to resolve upsets and disputes and maintain family unity.*
- *Create alignment through a common purpose and shared vision.*
- *Create an infrastructure within each family to encourage and support each generation to pursue their own individual path towards success and fulfilment.*
- *Create a culture of learning and development within the family.*
- *Intentionally prepare each generation to live effectively with wealth.*
- *Work together to retain and develop a families assets and their unity so that future generations can benefit from these same opportunities.*

We look forward to helping you face and facilitate a structured process that enables your family to work together to create your chosen future.

| **Brian Seaman** | **Cameron Thornton** | **Marty Chiu** |
| 714.352.0380 | 818.281.2360 | 714.931.1930 |

The ACU Foundation

CREATING PARTNERSHIPS OF LEGACY

For Individuals, Families, and Charities

ACUF Professionals are available to provide counsel and assistance in:

- Identifying and articulating your personal and family Legacy
- Preserving and transmitting values, character traits, and stewardship of time, talent and resources from the current generation to future generations
- Designing specialized financial and estate plans for the realization of personal, family and charitable goals

❖

Contact The ACU Foundation for a personal appointment to explore what Legacy Planning can mean to you and your family. All communication is confidential, free of charge, and without obligation.

The ACU Foundation
1949 ACU Drive, Abilene, TX 79601
(325) 674-2508; (800)979-1906
www.theacufoundation.org
Email: garrettd@acu.edu